VOICES OF
Gallipoli

By the same author

VOICES OF
Gallipoli

Maurice Shadbolt

HODDER AND STOUGHTON
AUCKLAND LONDON SYDNEY TORONTO

To Vic Nicholson,
who lived to see the day.

Copyright © 1988 Maurice Shadbolt
First published 1988
ISBN 0 340 431369

Typeset by Acorn Graphics Ltd, Auckland.
Printed and bound in Hong Kong for Hodder & Stoughton Ltd,
44-46 View Road, Glenfield, Auckland, New Zealand.

Contents

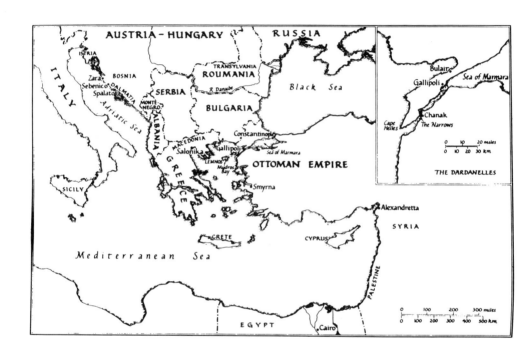

ITALY
ISTRIA
Zara
Sebenico
Spalato
DALMATIA
BOSNIA
MONTE-NEGRO
Adriatic Sea
ALBANIA
AUSTRIA - HUNGARY
SERBIA
TRANSYLVANIA
ROUMANIA
R. Danube
BULGARIA
RUSSIA
Black Sea
MACEDONIA
Salonika
GREECE
LEMNOS
Mudros
Bay
Constantinople
Gallipoli
Sea of Marmara
OTTOMAN EMPIRE
Smyrna
SICILY
CRETE
Mediterranean Sea
CYPRUS
Alexandretta
SYRIA
PALESTINE
EGYPT
Cairo

Bulair
Gallipoli
Sea of Marmara
Cape
Helles
Chanak
The Narrows

0   10   20 miles
0   10   20   30 km

THE DARDANELLES

0   100   200   300 miles
0   100   200   300   400   500 km

Introduction

This book is largely a collection of narratives which tell how humble and mostly simple New Zealanders lived and died on Turkey's Gallipoli peninsula for eight months in the year of 1915. They are the stories of old soldiers told nearly seven decades after the last shot in the campaign was fired. In the early 1980s, when they told them, the generals were long in the grave, the colonels, the majors and the captains too; not even a New Zealand lieutenant was left alive.

The Gallipoli peninsula — as half a hundred historians have been at pains to remind us — rises dourly across the water from Homer's Troy. It is as if the sergeants, corporals and privates of Agamemnon's host alone had survived to tell of Troy's fall. Theirs would not have been the song Homer sang; they would have remembered no dramatic deeds and duels, no Achilles, Hector, or Odysseus. Possibly they would have recalled their war much as aged and often still angry warriors do in these pages — as a blind, brutish and altogether inglorious campaign planned by posturing louts and orchestrated by elegant lunatics. Those who wish for a dispassionate account of the Gallipoli campaign of 1915 had best look elsewhere.

This book has mixed beginnings. As a novelist and as a New Zealander I had been fascinated by the campaign long before I first visited the peninsula in 1977. I grew up in a small New Zealand town which, in the 1930s and 1940s, was still in grief from the Gallipoli disaster, where the names of lost sons, husbands and fathers were thick on the town war memorial. As a boy scout I shivered through dawn parades on 25 April, the anniversary of the landing on the peninsula. From fathers of school friends, men who *had* survived, I heard of locations like Quinn's Post and Chunuk Bair — names which feature conspicuously in these pages.

Later, much later, I read most of the formal histories; somewhere in the back of my mind was the notion of a panoramic novel which would take in the whole enterprise.

That novel foundered without a whimper as I climbed the precipitous heights above Anzac Cove, walked the silent cemeteries of the peninsula, and finally stood on the height called Chunuk Bair. For New Zealanders sensitive to their nation's history Gallipoli is an emotional ambush. By day's end my wife and I spoke to each other in whispers. 'Those who return to the peninsula to keep an appointment with the dead,' wrote historian John North of such as ourselves, 'intrude upon its loneliness, its shattering silences.'

Our rendezvous was with the nearly 3000 New Zealanders whose remains reside there. Martial debris rattled away underfoot; so did human bone. There is possibly no battlefield in the world more extravagantly haunted. At first we attempted reverent burial of human remains. Then the task became too huge. For every bone buried there were ten more to inter. The rains of winter still wash hundreds of skeletons out of the melancholy terrain. They may for another thousand years. I recall only one experience like it, a visit to the site of Auschwitz concentration camp, where human remains were still ankle deep in 1959. As it happens, Anzac Cove *was* something of a concentration camp: 400 acres of inhospitable hill and gully in which 30,000 Australians and New Zealanders were cooped for months, dying from shell, shot, dysentery and despair. Mariners claimed that they steered their way into Anzac Cove, even on the darkest night, by the rising stench of unburied bodies.

Next day my wife and I travelled across the Dardanelles to Troy. Walking among the ruins excavated by Schliemann in the late nineteenth century we finally found ourselves standing in a classical theatre. It was there — with Homer hovering, not to speak of Aeschylus, Sophocles and Euripides and all those who have drawn on the *Iliad* for 2700 years — that I was struck by something extraordinary. No significant poem, song, novel or painting — literally nothing in our nation's cultural life — enshrined the New Zealand experience of the Gallipoli campaign; and this though Anzac Day, 25 April, remained conspicuous on our calendars. Was the experience too devastating, too disillusioning? Or had cloying sentimentality killed the imagination? Why hadn't a creative New Zealander — just one — ever found something worth saying about it?

In that theatre in Troy I conceived a theatrical piece — some kind of living memorial — which would allow Gallipoli to give up its New Zealand dead. Not a novel; a play. My first, and possibly my last. In 1981 I began research. I read through memoirs of the campaign, letters, soldiers' diaries. I did not approach any of the tiny and diminishing band of Gallipoli survivors. (In 1981 the youngest would have been at least 86 years old.) I felt — mistakenly, as it turned out — that their experience of the campaign was far too distant in time; that they might be too enfeebled to give a coherent account of battles far gone. Then I began writing. I wanted to distil the entire New Zealand experience of the campaign between dawn and dusk in a single day — 8 August 1915, the day 700 or 800 soldiers of the Wellington Infantry Battalion took the summit of Chunuk Bair from the Turks and for a few minutes had sight of the Dardanelles, the objective of the Allied offensive. It was the only occasion when that offensive came near triumph. Insofar as it was a success, it was the work of a few hundred ragged and skeletal New Zealanders. A mere seventy or so were to survive the summit. Of that bitter remnant, one historian wrote: 'Their uniforms were torn, their knees broken. They had had no water since the morning; they could talk only in whispers; their eyes were sunken; some broke down and cried like children.'

That day on Chunuk Bair was central to the New Zealand experience of Gallipoli. Afterwards the disillusion of New Zealanders with things British knew no limits. In a negative sense, at least, it was a nation-making experience. Arguably it was in a positive sense too: it has been seen as New Zealand's cruellest and finest hour. 'How men were to die on Chunuk Bair was determined largely by how men and women had lived on the farms and in the towns of New Zealand,' insisted Gallipoli survivor Ormond Burton, soldier turned militant pacifist, in his book *The Silent Division* in 1935. 'The way men died on Chunuk Bair is shaping the deeds yet to be done by generations still unborn in this land of ours ... When the August fighting died down there was no question but that New Zealanders had commenced to realise themselves as a nation.' Well, yes; well, no. But if there were any justice, 8 August would long have been a national day. It is certainly of far more significance than Anzac Day, the day when the dead of our wars in this century are mourned. 25 April belongs to the Australians, who first landed and established themselves on the peninsula. 8 August was the day New Zealanders lost their innocence. Since the 1930s Chunuk Bair had virtually dropped out of the nation's vocabulary. I wanted to restore it.

I finished a rough draft of the play on the eve of Anzac Day, 1981. The same day, at a publisher's launching party — at Waiouru military museum for Michael King's book *New Zealanders at War* — I met a rather diffident and shy regular soldier, Major (now Colonel) Christopher Pugsley. His first words were: 'I hear you are writing a play about Gallipoli.' 'Trying to,' I agreed. He explained: 'I'm trying to write a history of the campaign.' Jung would see synchronicity. Others might see fate. Here, with magical timing, was a man who knew more about the Gallipoli campaign than any New Zealander living. For the second draft of my play he contributed information, detail, and most importantly the diaries of Colonel William George Malone, commander of the Wellingtons on Chunuk Bair. The result was *Once on Chunuk Bair*, first produced by Auckland's Mercury Theatre on the eve of Anzac Day, 1982, admirably directed by Ian Mune and played by a bakers' dozen of male actors for all it was worth. But there was another and electrifying shaper of the play too — Chris Pugsley, who generously shared his knowledge of the campaign with playwright, director and actors. He travelled 300 miles up from Waiouru military camp to rehearse the actors; and was back again to congratulate them on their authenticity on the first night.

During the play's run I had an approach from Allan Martin, the director-general of Television New Zealand, to consider working on a television documentary of the campaign, as seen through New Zealand eyes. The prospect was tempting, but I thought not; I'd had my say on Gallipoli and now had a novel to get on with. Martin was persistent. Would I come and talk to him about it? I did. He explained that he would produce the documentary personally, and for sentimental reasons (his father had served in the campaign). If I wouldn't consider the writing of a script, would I at least consider making myself available to interview survivors of the campaign for the documentary? And the sooner the better. There were fewer than 200 New Zealand survivors of the peninsula left, and of them perhaps only one or two dozen able to talk with authority about the major events in the campaign. With authority? Yes, he assured me; a team of researchers had already located several such veterans.

Martin's offer was difficult to refuse. For one thing, I was then revising *Once on Chunuk Bair* for publication and future productions. Interviews with veterans might give me more material to work with, especially in terms of stage business. So I made Martin a proposition. If he could get Chris Pugsley leave from the army, I would do the interviews in tandem with him. Chris could take up martial issues; I could ask the human questions. We conducted our first interviews in June 1982. Perhaps two out of the first seven interviews were failures; the rest were extraordinary. These old men, near death, had been waiting for decades to tell their story. No one had ever come near them: it seemed no one was really interested. Suddenly there was too much to tell. And there was always too little time. We were conducting a smash and grab raid on history, literally snatching stories from the grave. Within two or three months the first of our informants was dead; within two or three years most were. By 1988 virtually all were.

The interviews — conducted wherever the veterans were resident, in familiar surroundings — went to a pattern. In most cases, this meant stepping back into a world approximating New Zealand before 1914 — an older, largely vanished, half-rural society. Living-room furnishings were dark, heavy, and Victorian: there was lace on the table, yellowing rugby team portraits on the wall, ferns in sunless corners. There would be tea and farmhouse scones fresh from the oven. The old men would be sitting up in dark suit and tie to tell their story; only their Sunday best was good enough for the terror, torments and griefs they were waiting to disclose. Most had been ready for hours before our arrival. Often wives were still alive. If not, tea was served by proud and solicitous daughters or granddaughters.

Few of the womenfolk had heard their husbands, fathers or grandfathers talk much of Gallipoli before, aside from a few commonplaces and perhaps curses. The New Zealand to which men returned after World War I hadn't, by and large, wanted to hear their story. If they couldn't talk pious, patriotic and conventional cant about the campaign, their fellow New Zealanders didn't want to know. They had learned, most of them, *not* to talk honestly. And here suddenly — at the end of their lives — was someone persuading them to do just that. Sometimes they baulked at questions with astonishment: 'Do you really want me to tell what it was like?' was a familiar response. Or, 'Mightn't this be too tough?' The more truthful the better, we assured them.

Television needed pungent quotes which could be stitched together in narrative form. Winning such highlights took time and patience. The old men had to be talked toward — talked *into* — 1915 again. That could take up ten minutes, an entire roll of costly film. Some of the more long-winded anecdotes lasted easily that. Pinned to particulars, however — asked how they had survived in a location like Quinn's Post, say — they often revealed total recall of Gallipoli's landscape, and the hellish lives they lived there.

On the whole, we managed not to ask questions to which we knew the answers; we asked those to which we didn't. That meant keeping to the battlefield itself. There was good reason for keeping to the point. Some veterans were only good for twenty minutes of interview; their voices would fall poignantly away, their memories fail. Nevertheless, we soon had nearly eighteen hours of filmed interviews. At that point Allan Martin began to pale at the cost. 'Don't we have enough now?' he pleaded. I argued him into more extravagance; I insisted that posterity would find it risible if we failed to carry through our programme of interviews, and make a unique record, for the sake of a few thousand dollars.

Posterity was never put to the test. Martin wearily agreed to let the interviews continue, and we went on to compile a chronicle of the campaign which was never going to be packaged comfortably in a television documentary. Listening to the interviews on tape, watching them on film, and then correcting transcripts, I saw that, in most cases, we had won more than highlights. Though the old soldiers talked in fits and starts, wove in and out of anecdotes and often wandered far from the point, there were the makings of entire narratives in the interviews. And that is how, five or six years later, they now appear here. Other than for continuity — moving soldiers from location to location, say — and sometimes for clarity, there have been no changes made: these, though reshuffled into sequence, are the stories they told, in their words.

The rest of the story is worth telling only because it demonstrates the difficulty of telling the truth about Gallipoli even now. Against my better judgement, but with prompting from Chris Pugsley, I accepted Allan Martin's original proposition: to write the script for the documentary, with Chris as my military adviser. I determined to base my script on the interviews.

Soon after, at a script conference, Martin disclosed that a former general, Sir Leonard Thornton, would be presenter of the programme. Up to that point I had assumed that a professional actor — perhaps Roy Billing, grandson of a Gallipoli survivor, the creator of the role of Colonel Connolly in *Once on Chunuk Bair*, and knowledgeable about the campaign — might most effectively front the documentary. Given that the Gallipoli story is one of high command failure, it seemed rather odd that a general should be fronting the programme. More so when it became apparent that Sir Leonard, recently known for his remarkably uncritical television series on General Sir Bernard Freyberg, knew next to nothing about Gallipoli.

After he joined the team skirmishes began on points of detail. On the whole, he appeared open to persuasion: Chris Pugsley and I had marshalled our facts convincingly. In any case the thrust of the programme would be with the old men, rather than with anything the presenter uttered. Or such was my hope. From the outset I had seen the story as human in dimension, a New Zealand tragedy: that was how I first knew it, in a small New Zealand town, and that was how I wanted to tell it here. But Sir Leonard was determined to see it — and diminish it — as a martial saga. For me Gallipoli had no more military significance than a lethal bar-room brawl. The differences of approach came to a head at a script conference where Sir Leonard wanted a line implying that one or two of our veterans might not altogether be reliable witnesses

— might not, in short, be telling the truth. I refused to oblige with such a line. Sir Leonard, of course, was not familiar with the hospitality we had accepted in winning the interviews, of the anguish we had encountered, the old men twitching with sorrow and anger, their tearful wives and daughters hiding their grief in the kitchen while we filmed. ('Why didn't Dad ever tell us about what he went through?' they asked. Indeed, why hadn't he? If we didn't give him his say now there was no point in the exercise.)

Perhaps here and there some had failures of memory. Perhaps too, after seventy years, one or two were now careless with the truth. On the other hand, truth had been rather careless with them. For a general, of all people, to suggest that these old soldiers were dubious witnesses would be like kicking them in the face — and their wives and daughters. My worst fears confirmed, I came close to walking out on the project and leaving Television New Zealand minus a script. Had it not been for my understanding with Chris Pugsley, and my desire to defend our research, I probably would have gathered up my script and departed.

Another significant exchange suggested the way things were likely to go. In discussion of the script, I proposed flippantly that the truth of Gallipoli had been hidden for seventy years because of the Great New Zealand Seemliness. 'Or,' said Sir Leonard, with evident approval, 'the Great New Zealand Teamliness.' It seemed this team man was still for playing it tight: sleeping dogs might be woken to mutter, perhaps even to whimper, but not to howl.

There was another intriguing exchange. For fifty years New Zealanders had not been told that many of their fellow countrymen on the height of Chunuk Bair, including the stoic Colonel Malone, had fallen to British guns rather than Turkish bayonets. It was disclosed in print for the first time in 1965, not in New Zealand but in a London-published history of the campaign, written by a Conservative British Member of Parliament. My script stressed this irony. Sir Leonard, an old artilleryman, objected. 'It happens,' he argued, 'all the time in war.'

'In that case,' I replied, 'should not the New Zealand public be told what happens all the time in war?' Evidently not. The incident — Gallipoli's best-kept secret for five decades — was later dropped from the script, presumably because of Sir Leonard's objection to the disclosure; it was information New Zealanders could still not be trusted with in the 1980s.

With my script finished, a Television New Zealand team of six set out for the Gallipoli peninsula. For the first week of filming I was a baffled spectator. Months of meticulous research, of careful selection of anecdote and incident, began to seem wasted. Director Doc Williams, as awed by the terrain as the Anzacs had been in 1915, tended to let Sir Leonard have his way with the campaign. It was plain that there was a martial coup in the making. I flew off to London, after stating my reservations, and left the team to it.

On the eve of Anzac Day, 1984, then, I had to watch the most expensive television documentary ever made in New Zealand — one so costly that it could only be justified by a fresh approach to the subject — inter the anguish and agony of the campaign under parade ground platitudes. My script had scrupulously avoided military cliche. Sir Leonard just as scrupulously reinserted such cliches — 'rhythmically' in the word of one reviewer — wherever he could find an opening; plainly they were more at home on his tongue. The Gallipoli campaign, in his version, had served 'to establish New Zealand's battlefield traditions' — which must have been news to the veterans we interviewed. New Zealand machine-gunners had turned their weapons upon fleeing British troops 'to stop the rot'. There was worse.

The largest sin was the distinguished presenter's attempt, after seven decades of romantic rubbish, to refuse New Zealanders a clear-eyed confrontation with their past. (Yet the Great New Zealand Teamliness prevailed again. As a member of the team responsible for the programme, feeling that I might yet perform some act of repair, I kept a tactful silence outside the privacy of my own home.)

Where the documentary broke new ground it was the work of the elderly veterans who had talked so honestly, earthily and painfully to Chris Pugsley and I through twenty hours of filming in 1982 and 1983. Not all of them were used in the documentary. One — with the most dramatic tale of all — was excluded because he mumbled. Another because he had a disconcerting facial twitch. Television New Zealand had no house room for the unkempt. Ours was the loss.

Chris Pugsley's fine book *Gallipoli, The New Zealand Story* (1984), derived largely from our year of research, went far toward correcting the record in other respects. But there was room for a book which would let the 10,000 New Zealanders who served and suffered on the Gallipoli peninsula have the last word. For a time I played with the notion of a novel narrated by a dozen veteran voices. Finally I left literature to its own devices and placed myself at their disposal as a storyteller. Here their stories are, then. Not my last word; theirs before the undertaker called.

By way of background, to provide a setting for the events mentioned in the individual stories, a summary of the Gallipoli campaign — derived largely from my script for Television New Zealand, to whom acknowledgement is here made — brings up the rear of the book.

Maurice Shadbolt
January 1988

The Men   TONY

Tony Fagan talked of Gallipoli in his small widower's flat in Auckland in 1982. The most sensitive, elegantly spoken and philosophical of veterans, Tony saw the first and last days of the campaign with the Auckland Infantry Regiment; he finished the war, after service in France too, with a nervous breakdown. The horror was with him still.

I was schoolteaching in Northland — a pupil teacher without any qualifications at all — when the war began. When I heard about the war, I went down to Auckland and joined up. I suppose you could say I was looking for adventure. Today people would say we were brainwashed with patriotism. Britannia Rules the Waves on our side, and Deutschland Uber Alles on the other. And now go out and kill each other.

Getting to Egypt, seeing an Eastern city for the first time, was very romantic. I saw my first fighting there. It was the Battle of the Wazzir, the quarter of Cairo where all these brothels and booze dens were. I happened to be there, on a day's leave, when rioting broke out between New Zealanders and Australians and the Egyptians. I got involved, though I didn't want to be. Liquor stores were looted, with people getting drunk, and then buildings were set on fire and girls from the brothels were crawling along ledges on top of the buildings. Then fire engines arrived and the soldiers tipped the fire engines over. Finally English troops fired down the street where I was. I sheltered in a doorway. It was a very violent, disgraceful day. I believe New Zealanders were wounded in the shooting. I arrived back in camp with my loot like the others. A primus stove and a bar of soap.

When we left Egypt for Lemnos and then Gallipoli we didn't know where we were going. Everyone knew except us. The

Egyptian newspapers knew. They published our invasion plan after Churchill's failure to breach the Dardanelles with the navy. I had my nineteenth birthday on the island of Lemnos. We were aboard ship in the invasion fleet waiting for departure for Gallipoli, and I had a gold sovereign burning a hole in my pocket. One has to celebrate a birthday. Three of us stole a duty boat from the foot of the gangway and rowed ashore to a Greek village. My sovereign bought a lot of liquor, and quite a variety of it, red and black wine and cognac and so on. The three of us got very drunk indeed and staggered back to the jetty and found our stolen boat. We fell into it and rowed out to where we'd left our ship. It had gone. A friendly Australian on another ship shouted out that ours had sailed out toward the head of the harbour. So we had to keep rowing, in a rather drunken and disorderly way, with sailors and troops cheering us on from the invasion fleet, until we located our vessel and were hauled aboard. Of course I was punished. They couldn't very well confine me to barracks or make me scrub decks, any of the usual punishments, not with an invasion on hand. So it was decided that my punishment would be hauling ammunition boxes for a Vickers machine-gun crew when we landed. That punishment was to save my life, as things proved. We turned in, slept, and our ship steamed away to Gallipoli.

When I first looked up at the Gallipoli peninsula, and heard all the firing, the rifles and machine-guns and big naval guns roaring too, I thought, well, this is no practice shoot. It dawned on me that there were people out there who wanted to kill me. I didn't like the idea at all. Watching the Australians trying to fight their way uphill, one became aware that war was rather a serious business.

Meanwhile we had to climb down rope ladders with all our gear, rifles and everything else, into naval pinnaces commanded by brave young midshipmen. They steered us as far into shore as they could. Then we had to leap out and wade ashore, waist deep in water, with rifles held high. A few of us were wounded on the way in by falling Turk shrapnel. Ours was the first New Zealand boat ashore, about eight thirty or nine on the morning of April the twenty-fifth. On our left, when we set foot on the peninsula, was the small headland called Ari Burnu. Two Australian boats had drifted toward the headland under direct fire from Turkish machine-guns. The Australians were lying dead in the boat and on the beach. It stunned us all, those two boats of dead Australians. It certainly shocked me. It was the first time I had seen death.

Our melodramatic Colonel Plugge, absolutely useless as a soldier, was shouting, "This way, Auckland." We followed up a ridge to Plugge's Plateau, as it soon became known. We had to hurry on, as machine-guns were badly needed on our left. The men carrying the guns and tripods raced ahead and I had to try and follow them with these two heavy boxes of ammunition. I lost the others in the dense scrub. Everyone just disappeared and I was on my own, absolutely on my own. It was complete chaos. No control. No order. No front line. We weren't even meant to be among all these hills and ravines and precipices. Here and there in this free-for-all were brave young fellows firing in the direction of the Turks or where they imagined Turks might be. There were also New Zealand bodies covered in blood lying very still in crumpled scrub. They were boys I had known alive only hours before. I began to comprehend what a beastly, uncivilised thing war was. Every shot I heard seemed meant for me. I was still trying to find the machine-gunners with my ammunition. I would drag the boxes uphill, then let them slide down a cliff and slide after them myself, and then drag them up onto the next ridge. Uphill and downhill, I made my way closer to where the fighting was. I found a small group of New Zealanders sheltering in a cleft in the hills and I was very tempted to stay with them. But I had to deliver these boxes. I could hear a machine-gun firing ahead of me and I made off in that direction and finally delivered the ammunition. I was told to go out on the right flank, through the scrub, and shoot at Turks pushing down Battleship Ridge toward Anzac Cove. My rifle was obsolete and hopelessly inaccurate, made in 1896 and used in the Boer War. I had to sight it for 750 yards to hit anything at 500 yards. Finally I discarded it and took a better one from a dead Australian. My platoon, which I would have been with had it not been for my punishment, was caught with no cover at all on the exposed ridge which became known as the Nek. They tried to dig in with entrenching tools but it was quite hopeless. They were killed, at least twenty of them, and their remains never recovered.

That was my first day of war. I was wounded on the third. I was detailed to move off to the right of the machine-gun crew and fire at Turks who were then attacking in short rushes. Whether I hit them I don't know but they were certainly shooting at me. The bullets were zipping above my head and clipping the scrub and I thought I had better get out of it. There was a dip in the ground just ahead which might give me more cover. A sniper must have had a line on me. As I jumped to my feet to run forward, bang, I was hit in the chest. I thought if one was hit anywhere but in the limbs one would die. What I did was say the Lord's Prayer out loud very quickly. My passport to heaven I suppose. But I still seemed to be alive. Blood was trickling from me but I was still alive. Until one was wounded one didn't consider death, even though one was liable to die at any time. That was because we were young. You don't consider death when you are young. Yet sooner or later I lost all my friends, and my best pal of all. Later in the war I heard blokes say they were going to die, and they would. They had premonitions, I imagine.

What saved me was my identity disc, or meat ticket. I had earlier taken it off my neck and slipped it into my left-hand breast tunic pocket. Though the high velocity bullet struck about a quarter of an inch below my heart, it was deflected by the disc in my pocket, so that it entered my abdomen and came out my left buttock. I crawled bleeding along a Turkish track and found two New Zealanders who didn't know where they were or who was in charge of them. They lifted me down into a sheltered gully and there, after a while, stretcher-bearers picked me up and carried me back to the beach, where my wounds were dressed. I was put aboard a barge which was towed out to sea by a pinnace. We stopped at two troopships and the question was asked, "Can you take more wounded aboard?" They couldn't. They were already full of wounded. Eventually we arrived at a ship which had some space. My stretcher was winched up and lowered through a forward hatch onto the deck below. There were 600 wounded aboard that boat, two doctors, no nurses, no medical orderlies,

no anaesthetics, and there we lay. I wasn't touched all the way
to Alexandria. I lay there without any attention at all with these
sticky bandages around me; they began to get a bit nasty. I don't
know how long that voyage lasted. Perhaps four nights. Perhaps
five. I lay looking straight up at the foremast the whole time.
I was one of the luckier ones. At least I had a stretcher under
me. Some had only a blanket. Alongside me there was a poor
Australian boy who had been shot in the head and was heavily
and bloodily bandaged. He was more or less delirious. Every now
and then he stumbled to his feet and waved an entrenching tool
handle and shouted, "Kill the bastards." Then he would fall over.
I was always frightened he would fall on me. In one of his sane
moments he asked, "Have you got a pencil, cobber?" I assumed
he wanted to write a last goodbye to somebody. But when
someone finally found him a pencil all he used it for was to lever
the tight bandages up from his head. Mucus flowed down his
face. I assume he died. The dead were just slung overboard. I
wasn't able to lift myself and see.

In Alexandria I was first in an extraordinarily good hospital
with Indian doctors and Sikh orderlies. When Indian wounded
came in we were moved to another one. As we improved in health
we were able to go swimming. There was one pleasant place, a
reef reserved for soldiers, where we could swim naked. Twice
we had the unpleasant experience of dead bodies, with bandages
trailing, drifting among us. They were dead dumped from ships
bringing out Gallipoli wounded.

While convalescent, I had the opportunity of returning to New
Zealand but I had this rather weird idea of wanting to stay with
the boys. In September I rejoined the New Zealand Infantry
Brigade, not on Gallipoli, but on the island of Lemnos where
they were resting after the heavy August fighting. They were pretty
shaken and silent, and glad to be out of it for a while. They
gambled — two up and crown and anchor — and walked to the
nearest village to take coffee and cognac with the Greeks. But
they didn't talk about what they had been through and what they
had done on the Gallipoli peninsula. No, they did not. Nor did
they talk about our commanders. They were all duds, all the
generals, including our Alexander Godley. We didn't think about

them. There was nothing to say about them.

But I still think about Gallipoli very often. In the last months back on the peninsula it was rather a romantic war. There was no hard fighting and no shelling during the day. We had each other's measure. We held our ground and the Turks held theirs. Flares would go up, red, white or green, and there might be a little fire from snipers. It was no longer a troublesome war. There were splendid sunsets with the hills outlined against the sky.

It was in France that I became over-familiar with death again. I remember finding a half-mummified New Zealand soldier, perfectly at peace, on a stretcher and down a shell hole out in no-man's-land. I often wondered what had happened to him and how he came to be there. Perhaps his stretcher-bearers had been killed. It was all slaughter and death and the smell of death and blood and people killed in the most fearful way. They were lying out in no-man's-land, where they would swell up for a time and then collapse slowly into the ground and mother earth would fold them into her arms once more and they would disappear into the mud they had so often cursed.

I finished the war with a nervous breakdown, or shell shock as it was then called, in hospital for seven months. I didn't wish to talk to people about what had happened to me, and what I had been through. You were well aware that anybody who had not been on a battlefield couldn't possibly comprehend what you were talking about. How could they understand? And what good was I, and what did I know about anything, after four years of that? I was lucky to get a job and somewhere to live after literally bleeding for my country.

Yes, I still think of Gallipoli. You may well ask if any war is worth it. You may well ask those lines of white crosses under which are buried the finest young fellows New Zealand could produce: Was it worth it? Was it worth your lives? No. No. It was not.

HENRY

Henry Lewis, talking in his quiet Auckland suburban home at Manurewa in 1982, was by far the most bitter of the Gallipoli veterans interviewed in that year and the next. The accuracy of his recall could be questioned; his passion never. He spoke with most authority about the cruel and hopeless assault the Otago Regiment, the 'bad luck battalion', made on entrenched Turks at the beginning of May. He spent most of four months on Gallipoli, from the April landing to the August offensive, and would spend his next seventy years cursing the campaign.

I was an apprentice motor mechanic in Wellington when war broke out in 1914 and I signed up to go away. I lost my mother when I was six and my father when I was fourteen and I was still living with my stepmother. She didn't treat me so good, so I thought the war was a good chance to make a break and get out in the world. Loyalty to the British Empire never had much to do with it. It was just a matter of wanting to get away with the boys. After I signed on I was sent down to Dunedin to boost the Otago regiment. I had five weeks' training and sailed with the main body to Egypt in October. It was very new and exciting. Egypt was all hard training and crawling over desert — rough stones, not sand — with our packs and rifles. When we were on leave we used to get in some strife with the English military police. Australians would come to our help. One thing we learned quick, we weren't English.

I still remember the name of every ship in the invasion fleet which took us off to war at Gallipoli. The landing was nothing like we expected. The sea was foaming with these Turkish shells exploding shrapnel down on us. Luckily, no man in our boat was hit; ours was the only boat I heard of with no casualty. I almost was. There was a man sitting in front of me with the barrel of a machine-gun. When our boat hit the beach and floated back, this man swung round and knocked me off my seat and down to the bottom of the boat. So I was the last man out. By then the boat was back in deep water, up to my neck, practically over my head. I had gear on my back and a heavy rifle which didn't make things easy. The first thing we saw on the beach was an Australian piggybacking a mate with his leg blown off. We were going to see a lot like that. We shifted to the left, and found it impossible to push up there; it was sheer cliff. So we had to make our way in the other direction, under fire from the Turks all the time. We copped it pretty bad, losing men right and left. I was pretty young, only twenty, and the whole thing was unrealistic to us, with our innocent minds. We began learning to survive fast, to take what cover we could.

Within two weeks of the landing I didn't have one friend left. I lost my best mate soon after we landed. We were very, very close. He was engaged to a girl in Wellington and in Egypt he used to read me her letters. After the landing he was transferred to the engineers. He got his gear together and set off across a little ridge to where the engineers were. One part of the path was prone to snipers. The last thing I said to him was, "Don't forget the sniper. Keep down as you go across there." I was sitting there watching him go, a lovely sunny day, and he walked upright. Oh God, I thought, and I yelled to him, "Get down. Get down." Too late. He was hit in the side. The bullet went right into his heart and he just said, "Oh God" and dropped. For me that was the worst incident of the whole campaign, seeing my mate shot like that. I almost cried. Without him I felt very lonely.

I felt even lonelier after our bloody mongrel of a general, Godley, put the Otagos into that hopeless attack on the second of May. Godley was never any use to us. Our colonel argued against the attack, knowing we weren't up to it, but Godley overruled him. We were exhausted, no sleep at all, and marched off our feet and pushed up at night into a deeply entrenched Turk position we called the Chessboard because of the square dugouts all down the slope. We had to haul ourselves toward them on ropes. I was way up on the left. I saw this little sergeant major, a Pommy I didn't like much, hiding behind me; he planned to keep me in front of him. I thought bugger you, left him to it, and climbed onto higher ground. From there I could see the Turks moving. The moon hadn't come up, the top of the ridge was all scrub, but I could just see the Turks crouched down, coming down, creeping toward us. To me it looked like some ruse. I sung out to the blokes below, I said, "Keep down. Don't get up here." But of course some of them didn't hear and the moment they got up that whole ridge where the Turks were became a row of fire. Every Turk opened fire on the Otago blokes who got up. They threw hand grenades too. It was our introduction to hand grenades that night. We never knew the things existed. While all this was going on, it was deadly. Most of the Otagos died straight away. Some of them just caught alight. The noise was terrific. You couldn't hear yourself speak. The Turkish fire was hitting a ridge to our rear and echoing back this way and that and we didn't know whether we had Turks behind us too or where they were. A bloke from another company dropped beside me and we yelled in each other's ears about what we were going to do. I said, well, throw away your gear and hang on to your rifle and we will gallop back as fast as we can. I said, if you get hit keep going if you can. Anyway we jumped back and found a safe possy, and we heard someone coming up to us. We had nothing in our magazines, on account of it having supposed to have been a silent night attack, and we loaded fast in case he was a Turk. This bloke screamed, "Don't shoot. Don't shoot." It was an Otago captain. He'd been hiding, sitting back safe, and hadn't come through with us. I was tempted to shoot the bugger.

When we took a tally next morning, after that attack, we only had eighty fit men left in our regiment. Eighty out of maybe 1200. That was what the first eight days of the campaign cost us. The rest of us thought we didn't have long to live either, and that we better make the best of things while we could. With every mate of mine gone to snipers, shells and shrapnel I felt very lonely among these thousands of men on the Gallipoli peninsula. I was the only one left of all the men I had trained with.

The war went on, though. When the Turks made their big attack later in May you didn't have time to think about dead

25

mates. You just had to hope you had enough ammunition to keep popping it into the Turks. I never thought nothing about killing Turks. Some say they were fine fellows, but I just thought they were a pack of bastards. They weren't the clean fighters they got cracked up to be. We knew they killed prisoners. They just kept coming at us. If any got up to our trench, we had to hop out and bayonet them back. Otherwise we just fired point blank into the mass. Our rifles got red hot, and some of them jammed. The bottom of our trench was ankle deep in spent shells. I don't know how long it lasted. It seemed many hours, but perhaps it was only two. I was black with bruises from the recoil of my rifle. There were bodies lying out in the hot sun, 3000 Turks in one particular acre. They swelled up to a tremendous size and turned black. Some had been there since the landing. Our fellows didn't seem to swell up to the same size. If we tried an advance, sometimes you could find yourself having to shelter behind the bodies and bullets would hit into them. The pong would be asphyxiating.

There was this armistice to clear the dead. Some of the bodies, you couldn't manhandle them. They were so rotten they were falling to pieces. The swollen ones, you just had to put a pick into them, to let out the gas, drag them to a trench and roll them in. But the smell never went. That smell was with you all the time on Gallipoli. Bodies were never cleared again. There was just that one armistice. It was a smell you can never lose. I can still smell it.

Our dead, the ones we could recover, were carried down at night to a sort of morgue down behind Courtney's Post. After men got killed we carried them down there at night where they would be laid out to be identified before burial. Passing there, you would look for faces you knew. And you thought, well, one day I'll be there too. Afterwards they would be carried off again and buried at the foot of a gully prone to Turk shellfire. There was one colonel blown out of his grave three times.

After the Turks attacked, dysentery did. I was lucky. I was the other way; I had constipation. But other fellows got to the stage where they were just passing green slime. The lining of their stomachs was passing out through their bowels. They should have been sent off the peninsula quickly. Doctors didn't excuse them duty. These men just had to keep going. They were so weak some of them just fell into the latrines and died there. They didn't have the energy to duck snipers and didn't care. I saw fellows commit suicide. Below Courtney's Post the path to the latrines was covered by snipers. You had to crouch low as you went along it. I saw men literally stand up and walk through upright so they would be hit by a sniper.

The food wasn't worth living for, if you could call it food. It certainly didn't do much to keep us alive. It was just bully beef and dog biscuits, which we made into a stew, with jam if we could get it, mixed up with flies. It was more a kind of porridge. Or a soup. After about three months we got mouldy bread from Egypt, one loaf to two men. We could just eat the crusts.

At the same time we began learning what it was all about. We heard the name Winston Churchill from the sailor boys who were bringing our stores ashore and taking our casualties out to the hospital ships. Those sailors called Churchill pretty horrible names, and told us he was responsible for the whole deal. First by failing with the navy, and then putting us onto the peninsula with the Turks prepared for us. We were soon blaming Churchill for all the thousands of lives lost. We never were free of Turk shelling. It wasn't even safe to swim in Anzac Cove at midnight. The big gun was always shelling from Anafarta — Farting Annie, we called it. When the shells started falling we would hide among biscuit tins and packing cases stacked on the beach. If it wasn't shells bleeding us, it was lice. The foot of our trenches were alive with lice. We'd cut our shorts back to give them nowhere to breed — they laid their eggs in the seams — and try and scrape them off our flesh with our fingernails. They'd be red with our blood. I was smothered in septic sores, especially around the crutch. Doctors would give us iodine, but they soon ran out of it. In the end they gave us nothing.

I caught a shell toward the end of July, and was buried in a trench, and dragged out by my feet. There were no visible signs of injury, but my back was hurt and I learned later that my heart had been affected in the explosion, and that I might only have six months to live. Meanwhile I just kept on. I got smacked again when the big push began in August, on the seventh, up towards Chunuk Bair. I was one of fourteen men picked to work ahead to cut barbed wire. The next day I was the only one of the fourteen left alive. I was hit in the hand. I had my wound dressed down on the beach and was taken off Gallipoli by hospital ship. Finally I was sent home to New Zealand.

I got sick to death of people when I got home after Gallipoli. People seemed so stupid, so smug and lucky, asking their silly questions. They had no idea of what we'd been through. No idea at all. They began making Gallipoli — my months there — seem unreal. I chased after quite a number of jobs, but no one would give me employment. I would go for an interview, and everything seemed satisfactory until they saw my discharge saying I was no longer fit for active service. They would say, "Well, we'll let you know" and they didn't let me know. Men like me were rejected as junk by people in business. I don't like to think about Gallipoli now, not any more than I have to. But most of it I can never forget.

HARTLEY

Hartley Palmer, a little lively man in his late eighties, talked in his home in the Nelson suburb of Richmond, in 1983. He had gone to Gallipoli with the Canterbury Infantry Battalion. Unlike many veterans met, he was not at all introspective or philosophical about the Gallipoli experience. What happened there was what happened, and for a fact. Though he didn't boast, it seemed apparent that he was as competent a killer as any man on Gallipoli. Some of his stories might have been polished in the telling; others were distinctly still raw. He managed to remain jaunty as he recounted the disaster of the Daisy Patch, and an act which would have been construed, had it been witnessed, as martial cowardice. But twice, as he told of the death of friends, his face crumpled, and tears dripped.

I was farming with my father when war began. I had been a volunteer with the territorials and thought I was sufficiently trained to go to war. So I enlisted. I was the only son in the family, with eight sisters. But I thought, well, I'm going and away I went. I'd heard fellows talking about the South African war and the times they had there. I thought I'd like to see what they're talking about. The British Empire wasn't in my thoughts; I didn't know a great deal about it. I wanted to have the trip around the world, and I thought it was a chance to have it. And I wanted to have adventure. You could say it was my ambition to go to war. I'd been trained as a good rifle shot. Sailing off to war with all the other Nelson boys made it even more of an adventure.

We had this strenuous training in Cairo and all of a sudden we were ordered to Ismalia. The Turks were advancing across the desert and they were going to use boats to try to get across the Suez Canal. They tried to cross the canal right in front of the Motueka platoon of the 12th Nelson Company. No Turk got across. My platoon was 200 yards away and I never fired a shot. But I could hear all the shooting a short distance away. There was only one New Zealander killed, and that was Bill Ham, the first New Zealander to fall in battle. We took his body from the canal and marched back to Ismalia and had a special burial for him. So Gallipoli wasn't my first action. Burials soon wouldn't be so special.

We had trouble with our boat and didn't land until well into the afternoon of April the twenty-fifth. About five o'clock. The wounded and the killed were lying about in all directions. I should say a thousand or more of them. The noise was terrific. There was a rattle of fire on top of the hills and the wounded was coming down the hills down to the beach. Most of them were singing out, "Have you got a cigarette?" Some couldn't walk any more. They were falling down in pain. I suppose I walked past thirty or forty dead. I don't remember being frightened. I was anxious to get up to the firing line to see what the others was doing. I never got that far. I was not into the main firing line, not in the first spell, not for at least a fortnight. The Australians and New Zealanders held a semicircular position at Anzac. We were posted to the end of the line, to the left. The next three days we were still in the same position. And we went out on to an outpost, just the Nelson company. It was there, on that outpost, my first mate got killed. That was Arty Fellows. I don't know whose shot got him. It could have been a Turk shot. It could have been ours.

Arty was the first of our company to get killed. I was about ten yards away. I went out and saw him there, killed. He was shot right in the head. He never said a word. My officer told me to search his clothes. I'd given him some money in Cairo and the officer said if Arty still had any, I was to have it. My mates said, "No good you looking, he's spent it." I said, "Good luck to him." I just found a little pocket-knife and I had it engraved when I went to England and I gave it to his mother when I returned to Nelson. We then buried Arty in shrubs on a little hill away from everybody. You couldn't dig a grave six feet deep, that was just impossible. Not there. We were lucky to get his boots under. I placed him in the grave with the help of some of me mates and one of me other mates read a poem from the little black book we all carried and that was the last of poor little Arthur. I covered him up and put a small cross on top of him. It just had A.R. Fellows written on it. That was all.

From the Nelson outpost at Anzac we were taken down to Cape Helles. The British there was trying to take this hill called Achi Baba. We was sent out to the left of the British position to make the Turks think we were going to attack that way. Then in the evening we went off to the right. We had orders to go over the top next morning as soon as British battleships had shelled Achi Baba. I suppose the bombardment lasted a quarter of an hour or twenty minutes. The British thought they had killed everyone but they hadn't. The shells fell too far behind the Turkish lines. The Turks were intact and ready for us. As soon as the bombardment finished we were ordered over the top. When we ran across the Daisy Patch toward the Turk line there was thousands of rifles and machine-guns trained on us. They were across open country just 400 yards away. We were getting shot from all directions. It was just a mass of bullets. The ground was hopping with bullets like it was hailing. The Turks was all in trenches. All you could see was their heads. They weren't in the open at all. They had every chance of shooting us and we couldn't shoot them as we ran. I didn't think I'd ever get to the Turkish lines the way things were. There was a machine-gun trained across where I was. There were five chaps killed in front of me. One, two, three, four, five, as quick as that. I went down too. I thought it was no good going through that machine-gun fire just to get killed and I ducked down and lay as flat as I could. With my entrenching tool in one hand I tried to dig in and all of a sudden I got a bash under the entrenching tool with a bullet. It just missed me arm. I felt the shock of the dirt. I put me entrenching tool over me brains and another bullet came straight at me. That bullet went down. I played dead in the hot sun until dark. Then I made my way back into the olive groves. Sixty of our company was lost. I managed to meet one of me old mates. He'd been shot in the foot and I helped him back to the doctor. That was what the Daisy Patch was. Playing dead with entrenching tool over me brains and helping me wounded mate back to the doctor.

It was a silly thing ever to think about. We knew very, very little about what we were supposed to be doing. We hadn't a hope of doing anything to the Turks at all. Not with the few men we had. We hadn't a chance to take Achi Baba in daylight. We couldn't advance into thirty or forty thousand Turk rifles. It was a bad act for any general. I suppose I mean Sir Ian Hamilton. He was in charge at Cape Helles. We couldn't blame General Godley for the Daisy Patch. He was still up at Anzac. We were angry to think we'd lost so many men with no gain. We never won any country at all.

So we went back to Anzac. At first we were huddled under the place we called the Sphinx. My officer said to me, "I'm ill. I've got to get away. Will you help me down to the beach?" I took him down there and when I got back my company was gone. I didn't know where they'd gone to. I had to go on my own to find my company. I walked over a hill and while I walked along I was getting sniped at by a Turk about four or five hundred yards away. I didn't know where I was. I was alone in strange country with this sniper. Finally I got down into a gully and saw a New Zealander I knew. I said, "Where's my company?" "Oh," he said, "up there. Up those steps you can see far away in the distance." So I went up those steps far away in the distance and that was how I found my company. They had taken over Quinn's Post.

When I got into the trenches at Quinn's I found we were less than twenty yards off the Turk trenches. Between our trenches and theirs were about fifteen or twenty bodies. They were there for the whole time I was in Quinn's Post, about six weeks. The stink was worst at night. You can guess how we lived. The biggest item living at Quinn's was trying to get a bit of sleep in the racket. You were lucky to get two hours of it. You couldn't sleep because of the flies. Flies, they flew in and out of your mouth like a hive of bees, and over the top of you. You couldn't drink your tea or stew a bit of food without the flies pouring down. Every bush you touched buzzed with flies. You couldn't see the open latrines for flies, flies thicker than anything you ever seen. We fought the flies harder than we fought the Turks. When I looked out my periscope all I could see was a heap of flies, not bodies, between us and the Turks. The flies were just about four inches deep over the bodies, that's what you looked at.

Above the bodies was the Turk sandbags. You could see that their sandbags were all loopholes. They had iron loopholes. We had no iron loopholes, so they had superior fire, with proper loopholes to shoot through. We had to make a loophole out of a sandbag and if you showed yourself they could shoot you through the corner of a sandbag. I don't know that I ever shot a Turk outright. If I shot them I shot them through loopholes. I shot at a Turk 700 yards away once, and he dropped. A lot of others fired at the same time, so I don't know if it was my shot. But I wouldn't have liked my shot fired at me. My old rifle didn't tell lies. I could put seven shots out of ten into the bull's eye.

There were night raids from Quinn's Post. A hundred of us went across. When we advanced a bullet fired from the Turks struck a dead body and rotting flesh flew up over me front, from me chest down to me puttees. I had to wait until the attack had quietened down to get meself clean. Stink wasn't in it when a dead body had been disturbed. One day I had a chance to go down to the beach. I hadn't had a swim in weeks. The lice was driving me mad. I took all me clothes off and threw them in the tide and I said to the lice, "Now you stop there, you buggers, till tomorrow morning. You stop there until I go back to the trenches tomorrow." I thought they would drown but by God they'd fattened. I pulled on my shirt to dry it out as I walked back up to the trenches, and they were suddenly crawling all over me body again. They said, "We haven't had a feed for twenty-four hours, what are you doing to us?" By God they was big. Nobody knows what lice and flies are about until they have to stand up and swing their arms about and swear like we did on Gallipoli. At Quinn's Post we was fighting lice, flies, stink and Turks. You didn't have time to get bored.

I stayed sane at Quinn's Post by always looking to kill the other bugger. Looking to kill the other bugger and looking after meself while I was doing it. I had nothing against Turks personally. You shot at everything you could shoot at. I went sniping in no-man's-land sometimes. I know I made the Turks keep their head down when I got stuck in. I knew my gun. I'd had it six years. It fired two inches out of true, and I can still see every shot I fired. I fired thousands of bullets. My gun just wore out ready to be leaned up against the parapet at Anzac where I left it. I don't know that I can dwell on anything special about the campaign. It was a waste of lives. I remember three fine schoolteachers killed in my section. What do I remember most? Me mates. Nothing much more. I went back to Gallipoli fifty years later and had a look around. I remembered me mates then too. They're almost all gone now, even the ones who got off the peninsula alive. All gone. That's what I dwell on. Those good mates all gone.

RUSSELL

Russell Weir, then eighty-seven years old, told his story in his Christchurch home in 1982. Cautious, intelligent, reflective, he talked around his Gallipoli experience as if around a great crater in his life. He began on Gallipoli with New Zealand Infantry Brigade headquarters' staff, but after a disciplinary breach was returned to the Wellington Infantry Battalion and the miseries of Quinn's Post. Enteric fever saved him from almost certain death or maiming in the August offensive, in which the Wellingtons were to suffer devastating loss. Protesting that he never wept — that soldiers on the battlefield never weep — Russell twice gave in to tears as he talked.

The year war broke out I was working in a stockbroker's office in Wellington. I joined up because I felt it a duty. Yes, I can say I was patriotic, with a great pride in the British Empire. But I was looking for adventure too. Egypt, when we arrived there after the long voyage, was quite an adventure in itself. I had things easy, being a member of headquarters staff. I managed to fit in quite a bit of riding and sightseeing with my routine duties. And I ate well.

On March the twenty-ninth, a month before the Gallipoli landing, there was a great military turnout, with General Sir Ian Hamilton reviewing 20,000 men. We knew by then, of course, that something was up. On the second of April there the New Zealanders had their first battle, the riot in the brothel area called the Wazzir, with the English shooting down four New Zealanders and Australians, one fatally. The next day all leave was stopped and the day after that we began packing for the big move. As we packed I don't think anyone realised that we were all going to be fighting for our lives in a very short time. I just thought to myself that this soldiering life was a great business, with one never knowing what was going to turn up next. I mightn't have felt the same if I'd had any notion of what *was* going to turn up next. But we knew by that time that Gallipoli was our eventual destination. We were handed out iron rations for the landing, biscuits that looked like dog biscuits, a small tin of meat, and soup powders. On the tenth of April we boarded ship at Alexandria. It was lovely to get a little sea breeze after the desert heat. There were something like a hundred troopships in Alexandria Harbour. On ours there were 1700 men. I slept out on the deck as we rolled and pitched to Lemnos and closer to the scene of our real work in this war. We were each served out with 120 rounds of ammunition. I caught myself wondering how many of us would still be alive in a month's time.

So we arrived at the island of Lemnos, just forty miles from Gallipoli. The first thing we saw were pontoons destined for the landing being towed by a battleship. I had my duties in Lemnos, and I was very pleased to learn that I would be accompanying the first New Zealanders ashore when the big day came. It was expected that we would be landing under heavy fire, but I don't think any of us, when we heard the plans, knew it was going to be quite such a matter of life and death. On April the twenty-fourth, when we finally sailed toward Turkey, we were all laughing and joking. I slept through much of the voyage and woke to violent cannonading. I knew we were into it then. Our battleships were peppering the Turks along the peninsula. The Australians had landed at 4 am and I knew I was going to be trying out my rifle on a new target very soon. I asked God to let me do my best for King and Country, and to grant me a safe return home.

Standing off Anzac Cove, we had our first glimpse of the kind of country in which we were soon to be fighting. Steep hill country, robust-looking cliffs — not unlike New Zealand at all. And, being young and foolish, exhilarated by everything, we were anxious to get ashore. We thought it might be over too quickly to see any action. We had a rifle, bayonet and ammunition, and we were meant to use them. Anyway that's how we felt until we got ashore. Elated. Ashore, though, it was pretty frightening. The

36

beach was enfiladed by Turkish fire, machine-guns as well as rifles. Turkish snipers seemed to be everywhere. And shrapnel was exploding overhead at a low altitude. And there were the dead on the beach already, not to mention the badly wounded. It became clear to headquarters staff that the quicker we could dig in, and get our heads underground, the better. So much for the quick fight we thought we might be missing. That was to be our lot at Anzac for months to come. Dug in, with heads underground, and heaven help anyone who wasn't. The shrapnel was deadly. People who boast that they felt no fear in such conditions are just imagining things. On Gallipoli, from first to last, I lived with fear all the time, twenty-four hours a day, not just in spasms. Sometimes you couldn't sleep for days, so you had plenty of time to think about what might happen. Sometimes you felt obliged to put up a fight against fear — you might start digging madly, deeper and deeper, to get further down into the ground in the hope you might be free of fear. You didn't think of brave deeds at all. That was all gone. You just did your job. Even when I first shot a Turk I just took it as routine. I had no particular feelings. He was there to be shot and I shot him.

One of the few times we weren't underground was when we were shipped down to Cape Helles to help out with the British regular attack which had foundered at that end of the peninsula. We thought it was going to be something of a holiday from the Anzac sector. By then, well into May, I was no longer elated about war, especially about Gallipoli. I'd seen it all as easy, a walkover. Now I was into the reality of the thing. And it was no walkover, no holiday even at Cape Helles. Nerves started playing up — there was the thought of being badly wounded or killed at any moment. You could see the casualty lists growing longer. You could see the dead being brought down from the heights and carried from the trenches. You could see men shot in the head, with their brains hanging out, yet unable to die. You could see men die suddenly, from shrapnel bursts, even while they were bathing on the beach at Anzac. Above all you were seeing friends die all the time. Comrades carted away with sickness or wounds. You felt a regret deep down, but didn't weep. Soldiers don't weep anyway. Mind you, I almost broke that rule plenty of times. There was every reason to be depressed about how things had gone. And Cape Helles was no great improvement on Anzac. I witnessed the big Allied advance against the Turks, and of the New Zealand infantry across the Daisy Patch. It was just a hell. All those bodies lying across fields sprinkled with daises and poppies — or perhaps the poppies were just patches of blood. It was somewhere around then that New Zealanders got the name of 'the white Gurkhas'. We took huge casualties, especially the Aucklanders. What I most remember about the Cape Helles end of the peninsula is leaving our trenches. We were relieved in the middle of the night to go back to Anzac. A Lancashire battalion took over from us. Little kids, they seemed, about sixteen. And they were blubbering, crying their eyes out. Terrified. We tried to help them by saying those trenches were safe. They weren't, of course. We were just trying to soothe those kids. That was a fairly disillusioning experience.

Cape Helles was also my downfall so far as headquarters staff was concerned. I hiked off to the French gunners. They were well known for baking French loaves and we hadn't seen any fresh bread at all since we landed. We gave them some jam, which they didn't have, and in exchange got some of their bread. I was slow getting back to my position because of spraining my ankle in the dark, in rough country, the night we were relieved from the trenches. When I got back to headquarters I was charged with being absent without leave, docked five days' pay, and reduced to ranks — referred back to the Wellington Regiment. It was my first black mark in the army, and I thought it rather unfair. But I also told myself I was very glad about it, that I was an absolute soldier at last, a real man. The truth is that when I arrived back in the ranks I was surprised by the casualties the regiment had suffered. Of the Ruahine section of the regiment there were only 64 men left of the 253 landed on the peninsula.

So we were shipped back along the Turkish coast to Anzac again. Even the voyage wasn't safe. One chap was killed by a Turk shooting from shore at long range. At Anzac there was a lot of mail waiting, mail from home. I read some of those letters more than twenty times. Then we were back to navvying, digging trenches in the rain from 4 am to 7 am, when the job was safest. The only respite was a swim on the beach, so long as you survived the shrapnel down there. Even fetching water was risky. There was always some Turkish sniper well placed to pick you off. Someone was picked off every day. We had donkeys to fetch water up from the beach. Invariably the stubborn little brutes would stop just where snipers were worst. We used language that would put all the musterers and shearers in New Zealand in the shade. Anything to get them moving again. Being so pinned down we were actually anxious to get into the front line, into the trenches closest to the Turks. Very soon we were — first at Courtney's Post, then at Quinn's. At least we could have a turn at sniping now, instead of being sniped at and unable to reply. Not that it was difficult to stop Turkish snipers playing the devil with us, officers and men alike. Ambulance men carrying stretchers were not immune. We would have torn some of those Turk snipers apart had we got our hands on them. The shrapnel could be pretty thick at Courtney's — once we got a shower of it just when we were brewing up tea. It riddled our billy-can and we lost all our tea. By the middle of June the Wellingtons were installed at Quinn's Post, a very steep place, and the Turkish loopholes only fifteen yards away. Quinn's Post was so tight that when anyone got killed, there was no way of getting the body out. And you couldn't leave bodies lying round in the summer heat. They were dumped in a corner of a trench, sprayed with petrol, and burned. You couldn't do it any other way. That was Quinn's Post.

Our casualties there were continuous, but they could have been worse still if it had not been for our colonel, Colonel Malone. He held us together in that situation, and held Quinn's too. Until the Wellingtons moved in there had been useless, suicidal attacks against the Turk line. Colonel Malone — so we heard — refused to make such attacks when they were ordered by General Godley. He refused suicide missions of that kind. And General Godley, so we also heard, threatened Colonel Malone with court martial. Malone still didn't take the Wellingtons over. He was a great bloke, a great soldier. Our casualties there would have been even greater had he not refused General Godley's orders.

I did some sniping. We worked in pairs. One shooting and one an observer with a periscope. Your observer would watch for movement. He'd tell you five o'clock, one o'clock or three o'clock, whatever it was, and you'd place your shot there. I was observer for Captain Wallingford for a time. He could pick Turks out at any old distance. There was no feeling of hate towards the Turk. More dislike of what they were up to — which was aiming at you. They were aiming to take your life, and you were aiming to take theirs. Would I say we disliked our General Godley more than the Turks? I don't know. But he wasn't very popular. I certainly didn't like him. He was too hidebound, a parade ground soldier. He was nicely dressed and very good on the parade ground, and no good off it. Never down to realities.

After I had been at Quinn's two weeks — on June the twenty-second — I went down with enteric fever. The truth is that enteric fever and dysentery was a bigger enemy than the Turks. In delirium I just lost one day after another — total blanks — and I was taken off Gallipoli and put in hospital on Lemnos. I had the most delicious meal I ever had on the boat taking us to Lemnos — bread and butter. Marvellous after hard biscuits and bully beef. But I had the most awful dreams. Around me men were dying by the dozen with the disease. Their groaning was dreadful, but one had begun to take no notice of death any more. I celebrated my twenty-first birthday — the third of August — still in hospital, but by that time even further away, on the island of Malta. All I could think of was getting home to New Zealand for my next. On the eighth of August, five days after my birthday, Colonel Malone and most of the Wellington regiment — most of my remaining comrades — were wiped out trying to hold Chunuk Bair. As for me, I never saw Gallipoli again. No. Though it's become very vivid in these last couple of years, with even minor details distinct, I couldn't talk about it for a long time. Not at all. For sixty years I hardly mentioned Gallipoli even to my own family. Almost as if I had never been there. But I was.

DAN

Eighty-eight years old, Dan Curham told his story in his sister's small flat on Auckland's North Shore. Though he was ten thousand miles and nearly seventy years away from the Gallipoli peninsula, his memory of his months there could not be faulted. It was impossible to believe that this soft-spoken, self-effacing man — with so shy and gentle a smile — had very likely taken more Turkish lives than any other New Zealander on Gallipoli; one estimate said hundreds. Though he would have been the last to volunteer the information, and in fact never did, he was once known as 'Daredevil Dan' and eventually commissioned for bravery while serving in the Wellington Infantry Battalion. No veteran visibly sorrowed more for the loss of friends, or for what he called the betrayal which took their lives. Dan's eyesight had faded. Nothing else had.

I was a clerk, working in an office at Wanganui, when war broke out in 1914. As soon as the news came I volunteered for the New Zealand Expeditionary Force. I had to get my mother's permission first, because I was under age. But she gave it. With me, it was a mix of patriotism and adventure. I used to read a lot, especially books about deeds that won the British Empire. There was not the doubt and questioning there is now. We were more simple-minded. Britain was a great power, and we were proud of all the areas coloured red on the map of the world, and loyal to the Crown. I liked going to the annual territorial camps in the same way as I enjoyed my sports, hockey and rowing. I found an old hockey club photograph, taken before the war, the other day. When I looked at it, I realised how many of us had gone off to war and how many killed. The Wanganui Rowing Club just about went out of existence because of the loss of numbers.

At that time I'd been training on machine-guns for two years, in the territorials. I liked the mechanical side of things. It was far more interesting than learning to slope arms, all the company discipline and drilling. So I was right away placed in a machine-gun platoon. There were thirty-two of us, sixteen men to a tent, when we went into training at Palmerston North racecourse. Of course things became rather more arduous when we sailed to Egypt. We were worked very hard there, day after day in the desert, with a few breaks to see the Nile and the pyramids. It had its picnic side too, until the Turks launched an attack across the Suez Canal and we beat them off. We heard a few bullets flying over for the first time, and got very excited. We didn't know anything about Gallipoli at that stage. We thought we were on our way to fight in France. That was what we wanted. When the British navy took action in the Dardanelles, trying to break through the Narrows, we heard of the Gallipoli peninsula for the first time, but we still had no thought that that might be where we would finish up. We just got a little bit interested in the place. Then the rumours started. By the time we boarded ships we knew we were either off to Palestine or Gallipoli. We were landed on the Greek island of Lemnos and put into training again there. We learned to climb up and down rope ladders, with pack and blankets and weapons, and to go ashore from barges. We became very proficient and confident in a short time. The weather was lovely and the harbour at Lemnos was filling up most interestingly with big liners, troop transports, and a battle fleet. By then, naturally, we knew we were going to Gallipoli.

Otherwise we didn't know very much at all, or what was supposed to happen, even when our vessel sailed for the peninsula. We only knew that we were not, after all, to be the principal actors in this drama. The Australians were to go ashore first. As we arrived we had a grandstand view of the British fleet shelling the Cape Helles end of the peninsula. There were great geysers of water going into the air as Turkish forts were bombarded. We sailed on another eight or ten miles to the site of the Anzac landing and anchored there. We could hear and see the fighting going on ashore, and there were bullets coming over and popping in the water. The Australians had already fought quite a distance inland. By then it was early afternoon. We were given a little last refreshment and then a tug with a barge came alongside and we had a chance to practise what we had rehearsed on Lemnos. We scrambled down rope ladders until it was standing room only on the barge, a solid mass of men. After about a quarter of a mile a bit of shrapnel began falling. The men on the barge made me think of Muslim pilgrims at Mecca. Every time there was a burst of shrapnel overhead we all bowed, as it were, each of us trying to get behind the chap in front. Fortunately only one man was wounded on the way in to the beach. We jumped into the water, clambered to land, and looked for shelter. The first casualties were being laid out on the beach, both dead and wounded. Perhaps thirty or forty dead were lying there in the open. The wounded were arranged under shelter from the fire and the Australians were trying to organise a dressing station. The dead didn't make me feel too happy. We knew then that things were going to be terribly tough. The hills ahead were stacked up one behind the other and almost all held by the Turks. We knew we were soon going to be uphill with the Australians among that heavy fire too.

Most of us managed to sleep that first night under the hills. The rifle fire remained distant, and there was no action perceptible. Next day, however, was very different. The Australians were entrenching on the top of Walker's Ridge. We were marched along the beach and sent uphill to back them up, into our first real scrap. The little we knew about machine-gun tactics soon became apparent. As we were hiking along the rough track up Walker's Ridge we heard the order "Machine-guns to the front." So the infantry stood aside to let us push forward with our heavy guns — Boer War issue, but still quite reliable. We puffed and panted upward, altogether breathless and exhausted by the time we reached the top of the ridge. And we were pushed forward, no protection or covering fire at all, to set up our guns in an open space facing the Turks. That showed the general ignorance. We were expected to expose ourselves to Turk fire in setting up our guns. Our officer was killed in the first seconds. Then one sergeant was killed and another wounded, again within seconds. Finally two corporals were killed. We were orphaned. We didn't get one gun into action and never fired a single shot. The rest of us abandoned the guns and retired with our ammunition boxes into the shelter of the scrub. Men were hit and falling all around us. Stretcher bearers couldn't do much to take out casualties because we were in full view of the Turk. There was no one to give us orders at all. And a lot of panic. Men wounded in the arm and shoulder, still able to walk, came rushing back from the line and panicked men lying in the scrub; they imagined the Turks were down on us and took off too. An Australian colonel threatened to shoot them and that controlled the situation. More and more New Zealand infantry moved in to reinforce the Australians and somehow the Turks were held off. That day, that second day at Gallipoli, our company lost forty per cent of its men. Some of them, good friends, old friends, were buried before I even knew they were dead. One I played football with, another one I rode with, a third from my Wanganui hockey team. School friends too, most of them. Boys I'd grown up with. They'd disappeared before I even knew it. It was an awful thing to discover they'd gone so suddenly.

After a few days we were taken off Walker's Ridge and reorganised, what was left of us. I was promoted on the backs of casualties — first as corporal, then as sergeant. As the situation stabilised on the Anzac sector, in the weeks and then months following the landing, we occupied outposts like Courtney's and Quinn's. Quinn's was such a restless place. We were practically looking into the eyes of the Turk, just twelve yards or so away. There was always someone, us or them, digging and tunnelling. No one could get a real advantage. It was always stalemate. We shot at each other and bombed each other and it wasn't very encouraging at all. Colone Malone made us work on Quinn's so that it grew from an untidy, dangerous collection of trenches into a really strong fortified post, clean and tidy and with overhead protection against bombs. He worked us to death until it was safe. If Quinn's wasn't held, then no one in Anzac was safe. That was the fact of the matter. We got no rest there and very little sleep under the stars. We could always hear the Turks coughing and talking nearby. And there was endless digging — the thud, thud, thud of picks and shovels just feet under our heads — and mines going off that weren't meant to. Not to speak of bombs hitting our chicken-wire protection to roll back into no-man's-land and explode. One of our fellows, I remember, failed to get his jam-tin bomb off at the Turks — it didn't clear the netting and fell back into our trench — and blew up in the faces of a couple of officers just arriving to inspect us. I dare say Quinn's gave them a lot to think about as they were carried away to hospital. No, there never was much sleep. And our food was never more than bully beef and hard biscuits. Men actually broke their teeth on the biscuits. No greens, butter or milk or real bread. Just a quart of water a day for cooking, washing and drinking, no more. And of course there were the bodies between us and the Turks, and the smell. There was a particularly unpleasant corpse — one of ours or one of theirs — right in front of our firestep which someone tried to burn with inflammable liquid one night, and that made matters worse; we had to live, eat and sleep with the smell of roasted human flesh for days afterwards. I suppose you could say Quinn's wasn't boring. We wrote our letters home to New Zealand, which had begun to seem a very desirable place indeed, or marked up those cards we were given, crossing out the words which didn't apply, and leaving just the message "I am well."

In the stalemate of Quinn's we knew there was no way forward, that we had to break out of the trap from another direction, through fresh country. That was how the assault on Chunuk Bair, the most tragic event in the entire campaign, came about. It was planned, of course, in conjunction with the landing of a division of British troops in Suvla Bay. The intention was to cut the Gallipoli peninsula in two, right across to the Narrows. But we knew perfectly well that Chunuk Bair was the key — the key, that is, to victory or defeat on the peninsula. That hill was vital. It dominated the middle of the peninsula and commanded ground right down to the Narrows. And in the August offensive Chunuk Bair was the objective of the New Zealand Infantry Brigade. Victory or defeat was in our hands.

At any rate the Wellington Infantry Battalion was taken out of the front line and spent a day on the beach waiting for nightfall. We were thin, most of us, weak with dysentery and poor nutrition.

I don't know how we retained fitness in cramped places like Quinn's, with snipers ready to take our heads off if we tried walking about. But we did. And morale was remarkably high. We felt we might accomplish something after all. We thought that not only might we make a breakthrough, but that we might actually win the war.

After dark we were marched most of a mile toward Suvla Bay and then inland. We were told to be very quiet, not to rattle our equipment or rifles. We didn't know how near or far the Turks were. We just knew where Chunuk Bair was. All of a sudden, in the dark, there was a very merry haka from the Maori contingent on the seaward side of the valley up which we were travelling. My word, it startled us. Then rifles began to bang. The Maoris, it turned out, were dealing with a Turk outpost. Word came down to us that it was all right, the Turks had been wiped out, and we could proceed uphill, up a rough track leading from the sea toward Chunuk Bair. We moved very slowly behind our guides. At one point they went astray and took us up the wrong valley in the dark, which caused much delay. We went uphill as far as we could, and some of us mounted our guns at a place called the Apex, about halfway up the hill, in preparation for the assault on Chunuk Bair. We camped there the rest of the night in preparation for the attack. The Aucklanders attacked first, racing into heavy Turk fire, and their bodies were left strewn in the scrub up the approach to Chunuk Bair. The Wellingtons, after that failure, postponed their assault to the following day. Two companies attacked in the early hours of August the eighth — there wasn't room for the whole regiment — and we machine-gunners were left behind at the Apex. Chunuk Bair was taken without loss that morning. For some inexplicable reason there were next to no Turks left on it. Colonel Malone established a headquarters there while men tried to dig into the stony ground on the summit with their little entrenching tools.

With daylight word came that the machine-guns were to go up. We decided that two of our four guns were to go up for a start. Though there then didn't seem to be much fighting on the summit, Turkish fire was mounting in our neighbourhood. I was to carry one gun. The track uphill was steep and hard going. We had just jumped from our trench and gone a little way, sixteen of us with two guns, when Turks spotted us and we met a hail of bullets. We made perfect targets. We couldn't run with the load we were carrying, guns, tripods, and all our boxes of ammunition. It was a quite deadly volley. Dust spurted up around our feet as the bullets struck the ground. I tried to lift my knees high to escape them. Men began falling around me. They just dropped, men I'd been living alongside, fighting alongside, for months; boys from my own town. We had been a very close-knit little group, almost brothers. But we couldn't stop or sorrow for the fallen. Our orders were to go on, to the top of Chunuk Bair. More and more of us fell. I kept on uphill until I discovered myself altogether alone, the one survivor of the sixteen who started out. By some miracle I was the only one who got anywhere near the summit of Chunuk Bair. I never saw or heard of my comrades again; I don't even know what happened to their bodies.

By the time I got near the summit, just with the one gun, no tripod, no ammunition, the Turks had reinforced and counter-attacked and were trying to dislodge the Wellingtons from Chunuk Bair. There was a terrific fight going on. Without tripod or ammunition my gun of course was quite useless. There was nothing I could do. Just throw my gun at the Turks, that's all. They were creeping up the hill under cover and lobbing bombs among us, and we had no bombs, no defence at all. If you lifted your head you were shot immediately. We just lay in trenches — hardly trenches, just scratches in the stony ground — and hoped the bombs wouldn't annihilate us altogether. It was an appalling day, a massacre, a tragedy from start to finish. Men were being killed and wounded all over the place. Otherwise it was every man for himself trying to get down under this dreadful Turk bombing and rifle fire. And I never even got near the front line. I certainly never got high enough to see the Narrows, our goal, as some of our chaps did. I stayed there useless all day, unable to move forward, unable to go back. Nor did I ever get far enough to see the bayonet charges Colonel Malone led. Badly wounded men from further forward crawled down among us, more and more as the day went on, and it was clear our numbers were down to a dangerously low level. Nearly all our officers had been killed, Colonel Malone too. Everyone had confidence in Colonel Malone — he was always an inspiration — and his death was tragic for us. It was said he was killed by a shell splinter, and as far as we know it was only the British navy doing the shelling that day.

We were more and more isolated, with almost no communication whatever, and yet we were still fighting, still trying to hang on to Chunuk Bair. I could see the hopelessness of it, the suffering, the wounded and the dying pathetically lying there with no attention at all. I felt disappointment and anger when I looked down to our left and saw that the British had landed in Suvla Bay, with all that open ground before them, and were making no advance. We could see them chatting on the shore with no opposition whatever and here we were, fighting and falling on Chunuk Bair, and counting on the British to move in and roll up the Turks. And nothing happened. Nothing. We were left stranded with no support. It was a total washout, one of the greatest tragedies of the war. When I consider the magnitude of our suffering that day — the Wellington men dying around, trying to hold Chunuk Bair — I still feel the betrayal I felt then. A soldier thinks sometimes, and that day on Chunuk Bair gave us a lot to think about.

We were relieved after nightfall by some British soldiers, untrained troops I think they were, sheep without a shepherd. They didn't know where they were, or what they were going into. I felt terribly sorry for them. As they moved in we moved out, what was left of our battalion — something like sixty fit men left out of more than 700 Wellingtons who made the attack that morning. When I got back downhill I was greeted as one from the grave. I still had my gun with me, and that was all.

A day or two later I stood to in the morning on Rhododendron Spur, and afterwards, since I was the most senior gunner left, put that one remaining machine-gun on a groundsheet, oiled it, and did all the necessary things to get it in working order again. Then the most natural thing was to try it out. I pointed it not up Chunuk Bair, but across to the adjoining hill, named 971. I fired little bursts and could see dust rising where the bullets hit. I was still fingering the gun when I saw the most amazing sight

— a mass of Turks surging down the hill, perhaps 600 of them, across the very spot where I had my gun trained. All I had to do was press the trigger and they fell all over the place. They can't have been much use as a military unit afterwards. The Wellingtons were no longer much of a military unit either. That was the day when the summit of Chunuk Bair returned to Turk hands. It was all over. From then on we knew there was little hope of victory on the peninsula, that all the suffering had been in vain. I didn't weep physically over the graves of my comrades. I was not a weeping chap. I wept in my heart.

I have felt their loss very deeply for the rest of my life, right to the present day. Talking about Gallipoli, especially about Chunuk Bair, brings sorrow to my heart even as I talk to you now.

GEORGE

George Skerret, a youthful and articulate ninety-year-old, talked in his widower's flat in Invercargill. He had seen out Gallipoli, in the Otago Battalion, as a member of the medical corps. Though he had perhaps seen more suffering than any other survivor interviewed — his battles had been with anguish and agony rather than with the Turks — he was at first perceptibly cautious, anxious to say the right thing. Finding sympathetic listeners, indignation began to come quickly; he would finally confess that he frequently wished himself dead on Gallipoli; that he had thought of suicide. His vocabulary was seldom adequate to his experience: he choked again and again on words like 'frightful' and 'terrible' and shook his head helplessly. Asking him to recall events began to seem as cruel as the events themselves.

I was working on the wharves at Bluff when war began. There was a meeting the night the news came. I put my name down as a volunteer. I don't know why I joined up. I knew all my mates were going so I did too. I wasn't thinking about the British Empire. It was more the thought of a bit of adventure. The last thing I thought of was King and Country. I'm pretty certain all the Bluff boys were the same. What we got was Gallipoli.

Our first sight of it was from the sea on the day of the landing. It looked wild country. Like some part of New Zealand really. We didn't land until three in the afternoon. Ashore, it was frightful. Terrible. I'd never seen anything like that before. We followed the fighting, until we were halfway up Walker's Ridge. I saw men with all kinds of wounds. Arms off. Legs off. All we could do was bandage them up as best we could and get them back to the beach. That was our main job, getting casualties back to the beach. It was a problem sorting out the living from the dead. We looked at each man fairly closely. When they could walk there wasn't any trouble. Stretcher-bearers took away the severely wounded. All we could do was bandage them up and give morphia pills to ease their suffering. Some died on the way back to the beach. They had to sort things out back there.

We dealt with everyone at our dressing station. Not just the Otago boys. Australians and New Zealanders were all mixed up at that stage. But it was a big shock seeing Otago boys. Ones from home. Ones you knew. I was very disturbed. The advanced dressing station had a doctor and five of us orderlies. All we could do was temporary things. Nothing very big or serious. Stomach wounds were the worst, though they turned out to be better than head wounds of course. We were fairly close to the firing. I don't mind saying I was afraid. Yes, I was afraid. It felt pretty awful. The Turks up there above, and liable to be down on top of us at any time. We were so busy with the wounded, though, we didn't have much time to think about being killed ourselves. We just kept going. We had a lot to think about later when we were back on the beach, when things sort of settled down. We talked about things, what we'd seen, and about getting home. I grieved. Yes, I did. About dead friends. Five Bluff boys I knew, friends, were killed in our first half-hour ashore. I remember one I used to play cricket with. A cousin I used to row with. A chap I used to work with on the Bluff waterfront. Another I boxed with. It was a great blow. When you saw them dying. When you knew they couldn't survive, couldn't live. It was a terrible shock. I grieved about home and my people too. I watched friends dying but I couldn't imagine myself dying. We knew what we were up against.

That was just the first day. That was just April the twenty-fifth. The second and third of May were worse, especially for the Otago Battalion, at the time of the big night attack. We had our dressing station in Shrapnel Gully, about fifty yards from the front line. It was the worst night I can remember. The wounded came tumbling down. All we could do was try to relieve pain. Terrible. Wounds in head, stomach, legs, arms. The worst hit was a boy I used to fish with on Stewart Island. A machine-gun had worked right across his body. Right across. He walked fifty yards before he fell. He walked fifty yards back to the dressing station and dropped dead. We didn't touch him. He was just one of many. Stretcher-bearers carried him off while we bandaged others and handed out morphia pills, slipped them under tongues. There was so little we could do with so much pain around us.

When the survivors of the attack got back to the beach they felt pretty awful about things of course. There weren't many Otago boys left. It was a bad night for the Otago Battalion. We got a bad spin. Some people said we were the bad luck battalion. We were, we really were. We felt betrayed. There was a lot of disillusion. No one expected it to be as bad as it was. General Godley wasn't very popular. It was after that day in May that disillusion really started.

On May the twenty-fourth there was an armistice. I was involved in that as an observer, nothing else. I wasn't among the burial parties. My job was to look out for Otago bodies. Actually I only found one. The rest were either buried before I got there or on the Turk side of the line. They put a line of pegs halfway between the two lines, each peg with a little strip of white calico. We buried all the men on our side of the armistice line and they buried all the men on their side. But that wasn't the first idea. The first idea was that we would pick up Turks on our side of the line and carry them over the centre line. The Turks were to do the same with our fellows on their side. This turned out to be impossible. You couldn't move the bodies. After three weeks or more in the heat and sun they were just falling to pieces. The one Otago body I sighted had a chest wound. He had blown up like a balloon. Other bodies had blown up and burst. I couldn't stand the stench. The burial parties just dug holes beside the bodies and rolled them in. But in front of Quinn's Post there were heaps of bodies. There were just eleven yards between the Turk line and the Anzac line and these heaps of bodies. They were lying in all sorts of positions, a lot of them swollen. It's amazing to think that they were all buried in that little patch of ground between the two lines. Just a space of eleven yards. They spread lime over the top of the bodies. That didn't do much good. It didn't do me much good either. The stench was the start of my dysentery. I was running to the latrines all the time afterwards. Eventually I passed nothing but blood.

Others were worse. A man had to be pretty sick before he was sent back to the beach. He'd have to be examined by the doctor. I escorted a lot of them to the beach if they could walk. A lot of them had had it. There wasn't another armistice to bury the dead. The stench got worse. There were thousands and thousands of flies. It was like living in a big graveyard, with bodies above ground instead of under.

In August, with the attack on Chunuk Bair, I was in a dressing station behind Rhododendron Spur. I only saw the fighting through a periscope. I could see the battlefield and the bodies lying around. Our doctor was shot in the dressing station. So was our corporal. I became the doctor. One man I treated had a hole in the front of his head and at the back too, yet he was still alive. The bullet had hit him in the forehead, then travelled round to the back of his head and wounded him there. All he had otherwise was concussion. There was worse to keep us busy. The best we could do for badly wounded was to push morphia tablets under their tongues. Our stretcher-bearers collapsed with exhaustion, there were so many to be carried away. Some of them got killed. It was over a mile to carry back the wounded to the beach.

I still remember the beach. There were a couple of thousand men lying there in all shapes and sizes and forms, all wounded and sick, and some of them thought they weren't as bad as others. We could only treat a certain number of them. The badly wounded, they'd say, you go and find someone else to look after, and they just lay there and died. Some chaps found an Australian and New Zealander dead in each other's arms.

I still think about Gallipoli quite a bit. It accomplished nothing. I remember the New Zealanders were taken from Anzac down to Cape Helles and ordered to charge across the Daisy Patch. That was just like going to commit suicide and that's what they did. Actually committed suicide by doing that. They were ordered to do so, and they did it. But it was the silliest thing that ever was thought of. New Zealanders thought more of themselves after that. They didn't think so much of the British. The British let them down. The New Zealanders felt betrayed.

I was frightened all the time. But we just had to go on. That's all there was to it. Forget about it. Or try to forget about it. And keep going. There were times when I thought I might be better off dead. Yes, I thought of suicide. I was just on the verge of throwing it in. Trying to get out of it. I dreamt about the horror until long after Gallipoli. Occasionally I still dream about it. Yes, sometimes. But very seldom. Mostly it's gone away now. Mostly it's gone.

In 1982 Harvey Johns was living alone in a small, sunny flat in Levin. A perky ninety-year-old, a writer of long-winded doggerel verse on the campaign, he talked quickly, with words tumbling over each other, in his anxiety to get his story told. Now and then he became breathless. He saw out Gallipoli as a member of the Wellington Infantry Battalion, a corporal rapidly rising to sergeant. With his mate Charlie Clark, whose story follows, he was also one of the few in that battalion to survive the battle for Chunuk Bair. He had been puzzling over Gallipoli ever since; now and then he drew a rather confused tactical picture. When he talked of Chunuk Bair it was very different: he still had Turks in his sights.

I was working as a carpenter in the Gisborne district when the war began. The day after it was declared I joined the army. I was as keen as mustard. I belonged to the territorials and we all had a little of the wild colonial spirit. It seemed to be born in us. And any war that involved the mother country, England, we wanted to be in it. Our country right or wrong, we wanted to fight for it. I remember us cursing and swearing, when we finally got to Gallipoli, because the Australians were landed first, on April the twenty-fifth. We could see the fight up in the hills, but we had to sit on our ship fuming until we were put ashore the next morning. Apart from a few shots falling, we landed safely, and got into a small gully. Finally we were moved to Quinn's Post. The Australians had been holding Quinn's and gave us to understand it was a pretty torrid place. You were in danger anywhere there. No one was safe with the Turks twenty yards off. Someone was always getting shot, killed or wounded. You would get that tired sometimes that you could hardly stand up and at night-time, when you were standing to, you would sell your soul for an hour's sleep.

There was always something happening at Quinn's. They were undermining us with explosives or we were undermining them. The Turks tried to train a mountain-gun on us. I watched what they were doing through the sight of my periscope rifle. We let them get it properly installed and fire three shells and then we got stuck in, two of us, and cleaned out the whole band of five Turks with the mountain-gun. We never heard from it again. I knew I'd killed. It was them or me. You did the best you could. You thought it all out calmly, callously almost. I was in a special detachment of six snipers. We would move round into different little positions where we might get a shot in at the Turks. You got that good you could shoot the left eye out of a fly. You could pick out anything you wanted to. We'd shoot at the top of Turk loopholes to bring down dirt and widen them up, to shoot better at the Turks behind them. We split bullets — in the way we weren't supposed to, as dumdums — so that when it struck it branched out and made an even bigger mess. The Wellington Battalion had a very good reputation for its snipers at Quinn's. Another thing that gave us a good reputation was Colonel Malone. The men respected him. He never denied himself anything, he got into the battle the same as anyone else, and that was why he got killed in the finish.

You got schooled up, hardened. You see your mate stop one and he might say, "Hell, I've copped it, I've got this, what's wrong?" If you were near you would give him a hand to patch up his wound. I was intensely interested in my own wound when I got it. You take it all unless you are badly knocked.

Chunuk Bair was where I was knocked, in August. The Wellington Infantry went up Rhododendron Ridge in the dark, after the Maoris and Mounteds had cleared the ground, at half past two in the morning. We went over Chunuk Bair and down beyond it, to a little bit of flat. It was considered to be a good place to dig in. There were just a few odd shots coming in from snipers. We were living in anticipation, right in Turk territory, waiting to see what happened. As light came we could see the Narrows, the Dardanelles, quite plainly from there. I said to one of my mates, "I wonder if we can make it down to those Narrows." It was exciting to see the Narrows. We could have gone right through and cut the north of the peninsula from the south. Mind you, it's just as well we didn't. We could have had Turks coming at us from two sides.

Another thing I saw was a Turk transport about 800 yards off, I thought, well, that's good enough for shooting. I'll try myself out. I went down sixty yards in front of our position and put in several shots at that transport. I must have been getting on to it because they went in round the brow of a hill and stopped there. I decided I had better get back to the men digging in. All of a sudden to my left a Turk came out and lay down and started firing at me. I had to back move the whole time while I fired at him. Then another one came out and another and another until I had about six men firing at me while I was back moving. My only chance was to fire for number one, fire for number six, back to number three, number four, and make the fire erratic. And I said prayers. That was the way I got back to the battalion to report to an officer. I said, "They are coming thick now." I didn't know it, but those shots fired at me were the start of the battle for Chunuk Bair.

The officer told men to drop their trenching tools and grab their rifles and get stuck in. Things happened very quick from then on. Some fifty Turks about sixty yards off seemed to be having a go at our left flank. And at least half a dozen Turks had got over to our right flank and got behind a hedge, about eighty yards away, and they were pumping away at us and having a glorious time. They were hard to see. The only way you could detect them was by the shaking of leaves as they fired. So you watched for the shaking and fired back, making allowances for the distance between the point of the Turk rifle and the man behind it. You couldn't forget those details. The Turks kept making pretty merry for an hour or two, with us shooting back, and then things fairly flared up all of a sudden. More and more Turks arrived and the battle got worse and worse and worse. Our trench was only eighteen inches deep, with earth thrown up in front. It hardly counted as cover. There was a dead Turk in front of me, at least a twelve stone man, and I got hold of him with one hand and slewed him round and pulled him in front of two of us and used him for cover. I was only ten stone, yet I shifted him with one hand. Phenomenal strength comes out on occasions like that. We were getting hit in all directions. When you were wounded the only thing to do was try and get out of it. I got donged in the foot. A bullet exploded in the arch, taking a lot of it away.

I was assisted out by a sniper while I was hopping along looking for somewhere to hide. When he got me to this gully there were about 300 wounded lying around. The sun was hot. The temperature was about 130 degrees. We were there all day, more and more wounded, without even a drink of water. No one was looking after us. As the day went on you would get no reply from men, mates, you had been speaking to just before. They were dead or dying. They just grew silent. The wounded were very, very bad. As nightfall came I said to a mate of mine, Charlie Clark, "Well, I am getting out of this, one way or the other." Charlie had a piece blown out of his leg and I had a piece blown out of my foot. So we started to crawl out of this gully and down Chunuk Bair. We were hurried along by the shrapnel falling. We stuck it out, crawling little by little, all the way back to base. We got in about midnight. Our ambulance boys fixed us up. I remember the iodine burning into my wound, something to make your hair stand on end. It probably saved my foot. It took eighteen months to get all the bits of bone and metal out. I tried not to moan with the iodine. Good soldiers don't moan. They take what comes along. All the men we left behind in that gully, when we started crawling down from Chunuk Bair, died there. Quite a number of my own company men were in that gully. We know they died there. There wasn't shelter from shrapnel in that gully. You had to do for yourself, save yourself, if you could. That's what Charlie and I did that day. We looked after ourselves. We were the only ones to survive from that 300 in the gully. The only ones to make it out.

We heard nothing had happened in Suvla Bay where the British had landed. We looked down and saw no movement or advance at all. New Zealanders did a fair amount of swearing. They were swearing at the system, the whole thing. At the waste of 3000

New Zealand lives. And we had no respect for our General Godley. He was an old English regular who came out to New Zealand years before. We just considered him a bumptious ass. He had no respect for the human being at all and he was army from A to Z. He had no tact and he was universally hated. I am just being truthful, he was absolutely hated. More than the Turks.

I left Gallipoli using a rifle for a crutch. I was eighteen months in England where they tried to sew my foot up again, before I was returned home. I had three years in hospitals altogether. I'm still walking on that foot. I suppose I felt more a New Zealander when I came back. Yes, I did. You were comrades in arms, that is something you can't explain, and when you get back to your own country, become married and settle down with your families, that feeling simply grows and it has that effect upon the whole community, I should think. I wouldn't have missed Gallipoli for anything, wound or no wound.

CHARLIE

Weeks before his death in 1982, Charlie Clark talked in his daughter's home in the Auckland suburb of Pakuranga. The irascible old soldier was fighting his last fight, gasping for breath, impatient with questions which might impede his narrative. He had just enough energy to say what he needed to say and no more. The rest would soon go to the grave. That day Corporal Charlie won the battle, if not the war. His recall of the Gallipoli terrain was never less than impeccable; he had precious and piquant detail of the Wellington Battalion's hours on Chunuk Bair which no military historian had recorded.

I was on a bush-felling contract, back of Gisborne, in the winter of 1914, when the war began. Funny thing. I woke up that day with this dream that England and Germany were at war, and that I was in it, and my mate Reg McLay too. I told Reg about the dream in the cookhouse over breakfast and we got on with felling. I was chopping away later that day, with trees lined up for a drive, and the boss turned up on a ridge and sang out to me, "I want to talk to you, Charlie." I thought to myself, you can wait till I've finished this lot. I was expecting a row, you see. So I worked another twenty minutes until I had the driving tree felled, the rest of the trees falling with it, and walked back to our camp. The boss was sitting with me mate Reg. Reg said to me, "Well, your dream's come true, Charlie." The boss explained, "England and Germany could be at war this afternoon. I'll come back and let you know for sure. What do you two want if it's war?" Reg said, "I'm going." I said, "Well, hang on a minute. We've got this contract here to work out first." The boss said, "If war is declared, and you want to go, we'll cancel the contract and I'll pay you daily wages for what you've done."

Later in the day the boss was back with the news that the war was all on. Right. We hadn't seen Britain but it was our second home. If Britain was in it, we had to be too. So Reg and I went down to Gisborne. We met bushmen from all over the district there. They were all out on the town. Reg and I felt like a spot too. So we had a few drinks and marched off and put our names down to go to war. Then we had our medicals. Seven bushmen ahead of me were knocked back with strained hearts. They thought I wouldn't make it either, but the doctors said I only had three bad teeth. A week later we were shipped down to Napier, in a boat full of bushmen, most of us sleeping on the deck. From Napier we pushed off to train at Palmerston North. We had a few weeks' training and then we were marching through Wellington with the bands playing, off to the war. Off to Gallipoli, as it turned out.

Gallipoli didn't seem the least strange to me. I been seeing hill country forever. Gallipoli was precipitous, but so was the hill country I'd been working on. I don't remember being afraid. There we were, and there the Turks were, and that was it. It was just a job to be done like that tree-felling contract I'd been working on out in the bush back of Gisborne. We headed straight up Plugge's Plateau for a start. Later we was trenched in places like Courtney's Post and Quinn's Post, right among the Turks. At Quinn's, looking out on the bodies of mates, and not being able to recover them, you got callous pretty quick. You couldn't be anything else. It was no use feeling anything else. We seen out the heat and the flies and the dysentery for months. We seen out the British generals too, and their mess-ups. We didn't hate them. We just treated them with contempt. We treated some of our own lot with contempt too, the officers that ran. Not our Colonel Malone, though. Malone, he looked after us, the Wellingtons, and we admired him for it. He wouldn't allow us to be pushed against Turk positions in daylight, the way British troops were. We saw how the British ran things at the Daisy Patch, when New Zealanders were sent down to Helles to help them, and we took terrible casualties. We didn't think much of the way the British did things. Nor did Colonel Malone.

Chunuk Bair I remember like yesterday. We set out one Friday night in August, with the Maoris and Mounteds clearing the ground ahead, Gurkhas too. We all had empty rifles. Bayonets only to be used. It was meant to be a silent night attack with no shooting to warn the Turks we were coming. Otago men had broken up the wire entanglements to let us through. When we got through the wire we were formed up to make sure our rifles were empty, magazines and all, and bayonets fixed. We started working our way uphill. Then we heard something that made us stop — thumping and yelling. It was a Maori haka. The Maoris did it before they rushed a Turk position. They reckon the Maoris captured around 300 Turks. When daylight came we met some Turks cooking breakfast and let fly, and they didn't last long.

Saturday morning we was 200 or 300 yards short of Chunuk Bair. We could see the sun glinting on the bayonets of the British as they were landed down in Suvla Bay. Nothing much else seemed to be happening down there. Meantime we had Rhododendron Ridge to work up and Chunuk Bair to take. The Auckland boys was called up, the Auckland Infantry Battalion, and sent first. They went up about 150 yards and then they were stopped by heavy fire, losing a terrible lot of men. They was pretty well wiped out. So the Wellington Battalion, all lined up and ready, was called to go next by two British commanders. It seemed we was just a few seconds from following the Aucklanders into that fire. "Stop where you are," Colonel Malone told us. I was standing just near Malone when the British gave the order. He was very stern and strong-faced. Malone told the British commanders, "No. We are not taking orders from you people. Wellington is not going up there. My men are not going to commit suicide." There was a big row when he refused their orders. Malone said, "These men, the Wellingtons, are under my orders. Not yours. I take all responsibility for them not going up there. I will take all risk and any punishment. We will take Chunuk Bair tonight, in the dark, not in daylight."

These two Englishmen threatened to arrest Malone for insubordination. I reckon if they tried arresting him we would have shot them. Malone just ordered, "Wellington Battalion, come back from that ridge." So we did. We were all grateful, and we thanked him. We knew that a lot of us was going to pass out if we tried grabbing Chunuk Bair in daylight like the Aucklanders. We knew that a lot of us was going to pass out whatever way it went, but it didn't have to be that way. We backed off, down the ridge, with all our equipment on and rifles ready, to rest until the attack. We was told it would be at two thirty in the morning and to get some sleep if we could. Sleep? We lay talking among ourselves, quiet, the way I am talking to you now. We knew we was going to go over Chunuk Bair sometime. And we knew it was going to be grim, that some of us was going to pass out. There was some there that did show they were scared. I don't want to mention names, but there was a Wellington captain who took off, who we never seen again after that night. He shot himself in the knee with his revolver, before the attack on Chunuk Bair came, and got himself taken off Gallipoli as a casualty.

After midnight the navy and the artillery hit the top of Chunuk Bair with everything. I never seen a bombardment like it in all my time on Gallipoli. The summit was just a mass of flame from the exploding shells. Yet some of us managed to sleep through it. I did. That was how exhausted we were. At half past two men came along our lines pulling our feet to wake us up and telling us to get ready. The lieutenant who was supposed to lead us up Chunuk Bair, I don't want to mention his name either, he wasn't to be found. He'd cleared too.

Anyway up we went. We charged the rest of the way up Chunuk Bair with hardly a shot fired. Halfway we had a breather and waited till the last shell fell with a whoomph. The Turks had mostly scooted from the top. A couple of machine-gunners let fly at us but their bullets went over our heads and we shut them up. There was one bearded old Turk, about seventy years old, with a gun on us. We had to shoot him, poor old joker. We got into the Turk trenches and walked up and down, a bit worried that they might be mined, and decided to dig some of our own. There wasn't a sign of any more Turks at all. We could see the Narrows from the top all right. We could see a road, and traffic moving along it, and the Turkish forts looking over the Narrows. We were really very interested in seeing all these things we never seen before, and with no Turks in sight. We went over Chunuk

Bair, to the drop on the other side, about a chain and a half, and were told to dig in there. We only dug down about twelve inches before we struck rock. Then there was a call for 100 men to go out in front, to form a protective screen, to watch for Turks and take the brunt of the counter-attack if it came. We didn't get 100 men, nothing like it, but I took my section downhill about two chain into the valley. It was better than trying to dig into rock and fill sandbags like the others were. There was Turkish gunpits there. So we settled down in these gunpits, about twelve of us, and had a game of cards. We put two men out on watch, and there we were happy, quite happy. Not a worry in our heads. We were right in a war, waiting on a battle, and dealing out cards. Funny about men in a fight.

We were still playing poker when the Turks finally hit the Wellingtons on the left flank. We never saw them coming, but all this time they was accumulating for their counter-attack. Suddenly there was a terrific volume of rifle fire and yelling. The two men we had on watch came charging back to us and said the Turks were coming through. We was going to be pretty well in the middle of the Turks unless we moved fast. My mates said to me, "Well, you led us down here. Now you lead us back." So I took off, back towards the top of Chunuk Bair, with bullets hopping around me, and the others following behind. I flopped down in a trench beside Lieutenant Jardine of the seventh Hawkes Bay platoon, a man as game as they can make them, and he yelled out to fix bayonets and prepare to charge, to counter-attack the Turks as they came. I thought, well, this is it. I was never too keen on a bayonet charge. I seen one or two bayoneted and I didn't like it. I didn't mind being shot, anything was better than being bayoneted. You weren't supposed to have bullets in your rifle in a bayonet charge, but I made sure I had. Faced with a joker coming at me with a bayonet I could shoot him straight away. There was always shots fired in a bayonet charge, regardless of orders.

While we were braced for the bayonet charge, Turks to our left and to our right now too, their shots started getting among us. I heard thump, thump, thump and it was fellows falling around me. Nine or ten of them, suddenly wounded or dead, all the jokers I'd been playing poker with just a minute or two before. I couldn't see where the bullets was coming from. Then I sighted a Turk, just standing up, shooting among us. I couldn't get much cover, not in a shallow trench, so I left my head and legs out exposed. I don't mind telling you I had a horror of being shot in the body. I pushed my rifle over a sandbag, got a sight of this Turk, and shot him in the face. You could see the flash as he dropped and his rifle fell. Then someone hit me in the leg with a sledgehammer. It was a Turkish bullet taking a lump out of my calf and smashing bone too. When I looked at it, the wound was so big I couldn't cover it with my hand. I thought to myself that's it, dropped my rifle and told the other jokers they could have my ammunition. It was time to get out of it quick and lively to somewhere safer. I pulled off my boot to have a good look at meself and knew I was going to have to get a tourniquet on my leg fast or I was going to bleed away. The whole lot seemed to be blown out, right up from the foot. I crawled back through Wellington men on the top of the hill who were shooting to keep the Turks at bay. There was some Englishmen there too, Gloucesters, I don't know where they came from, but they broke and cleared. My mate Harvey Johns, a really cool gentleman, was trying to stop them breaking, marching up and down and shouting at them. I said, "Harvey, you'll get your bloody brains blown out." Harvey did get shot soon after. I finally crawled down into this ravine, one of the first ones there, where the wounded collected all that day on Chunuk Bair. It wasn't safe, it was under Turk fire, but it was the best place there was. I got a tourniquet on meself and for a bit I talked to a captain of the Gloucesters who was ashamed of his men breaking. Especially their breaking in front of the New Zealanders and leaving the battle to us. He said we were the best troops he could ever hope to see. He was very good to me, trying to find me some water, but there wasn't any. Harvey arrived in the ravine soon after I did, with his foot shot out. As the day went on, with more and more wounded, Harvey and I had to slide lower down the ravine to make room for them. Soon the ravine was full of wounded. Two hundred of us, maybe more. It was terrible, terrible. No water and no attention and nobody could do anything. We were being shelled too as we lay there. They called it "the valley of torment". Men were all smashed up, and getting smashed up even more, and bleeding away. They knew they were dying. They were brave men. That's all you can call them. Brave.

I don't suppose the first dressing station was really much more than a couple of hundred yards back. Getting there was the problem. It might as well have been a couple of miles, the condition we were in. Harvey and I knew we had to get to some place of shelter or we was gone. That was our first instinct, to get away from it all. On top of the hill the Wellington Battalion was still taking these Turk counter-attacks. We could see it all from where we were lying exposed. Sometimes it seemed the Turks was coming right over Chunuk Bair, through the Wellingtons holding the hill, and down on top of us. If we weren't killed, we would be taken prisoner. That put the breeze up us. There was no point in staying around to die or be taken prisoner. But to get out, just for a start, Harvey and I had to climb from this ravine where we were with all the wounded.

There was one little track out of it, about sixty feet, up to the edge. We tried crawling up it again as the day went on, but we only got up it a few feet before we slipped off and rolled back into the ravine. Toward dark we started to make it. I remember a clear space, covered with scrub, and being hit by Turkish fire, and dead men lying everywhere around who hadn't made it across. Harvey crawled across that clear space all right and sung out to me, "Now you come across here too." I said, "I'll go out like a light." So he said, "What else are you going to do?" He was right about that. I used an old Turk cooking place for shelter and made it after him. We collected water bottles from the dead men. Their water kept us going. Slipping and sliding, we both of us crawled in the dark, on and on, helping each other, and we must've got back to the dressing station about midnight. It had taken us most of the day and half the night to get a couple of hundred yards back down Chunuk Bair. I never made a longer journey. Near the dressing station Harvey and me got separated. I flopped on the track and a man fell over me. It was Colonel Young, of the Aucklands. He told two English stretcher-bearers to put me on a stretcher. As soon as he was gone, the stretcher-bearers tipped me out and took off. Colonel Young came back and said, "Where's the stretcher? Why didn't you stop them?" I said, "How could I?" He found someone else to get me into the dressing station. It was another long journey back to the beach.

The mates we left behind back in the ravine, they're still on Gallipoli. Colonel Malone is too. When there was a roll call of the Wellingtons, after the battle, they reckoned there were only forty-seven fit men left of all the 700 who went up Chunuk Bair on the morning of August the eighth.

I got taken off Gallipoli two days after, on the tenth of August. I never was in any other war. That one was enough for me. It never did anything, never gained nothing, but I been thinking about it ever since, all the years of my life, most of all that day on Chunuk Bair.

JOHN

In 1982 John Skinner, an erect, white-bearded and meticulously spoken veteran, then nearing eighty-eight and still every inch the gentleman, told his story in a home for the elderly in Dunedin. A student of the campaign, with a second visit to the battlefield and long correspondence with military historians behind him, he for one had long been on easy terms with his experience of Gallipoli; he no longer lost sleep over it. His dispassionate interest in the tactics and flaws of the campaign seemed to have inhibited most personal feelings. There were no stutters, no trembles, no tears. A war was a war, and wars were to be fought. Even if it meant enterprises as suicidally confused as that in which his Otago Infantry Battalion was destroyed — and which Sergeant John Skinner magically survived — at the beginning of the campaign.

In August 1914 I was working on a farm in Central Otago, an isolated place, a long way from a post office, and with newspapers only once or twice a week. So I was a little late in learning that New Zealand was at war. I joined up immediately. It was the correct and proper thing to do. I wasn't looking for adventure, or especially to defend the British Empire. You don't have motives at a time like that. Either joining up was the correct and proper thing to do or it was not. I had no doubts whatever about the correct and proper course. And very soon, as these things go, I was in training, sailing away, and being landed on the Gallipoli peninsula.

Going ashore under fire made it difficult to win much impression of the peninsula. Our transport anchored a mile or more off Anzac Cove. A destroyer then took us halfway in, until the depth of water and Turkish fire made progress risky. Finally we were transferred to lifeboats and, under shellfire, taken close to the beach. We then clambered out and waded the rest of the way. I was rather amazed by how small and narrow the beach was. It was filling up with boxes of bully beef, biscuits and ammunition. There was more to the beach than that, of course. It was possible to see how fast the casualties had mounted since morning. Past the high water mark a great number of wounded men were resting on stretchers or simply on the sand. A few were set to one side. They had blankets over them. You knew what that meant.

We were under fire, of course, immediately we landed, and we were never to be free of it in all the months we were on the peninsula. Meanwhile we were taken up the highest eminence in proximity to the beach, Plugge's Plateau, and there ordered to dig in, which we did. We had one particularly lazy individual in our company, the laziest man I had ever come across. Rather than dig in he lay down in the grass and very promptly got a bullet in his behind. He wasn't our first casualty by any means, but certainly the most memorable.

On Plugge's Plateau, where we remained through that first night, we were more or less in the second line. Such outposts as Courtney's, Pope's and Quinn's, further forward, were holding the line against the Turks. With the fight raging just a few hundred yards inland, and all the racket, lack of sleep was a larger problem than casualties. Our exhaustion was dreadful, we were never to lose it all the time we were on the peninsula. The next morning we had urgent calls from Australians holding the front line. For the next three or four days we reinforced them on Walker's Ridge. That was where we first began to take casualties in number. In our first days ashore we lost 200 out of 1000 men.

We had worse to come. A week after the landing we were briefed for an attack on entrenched Turks at the head of Monash Gully, the area best known as the Chessboard. Like so much on Gallipoli everything seemed to go wrong. We were marched a great and tiring distance to the take-off point and arrived late. We were supposed to make our advance in daylight, but it was dark by the time we were issued with picks and shovels so that we could consolidate the ground we were expected to gain. Our first obstacle was a steep and gravelly cliff down which a rope was suspended; in the pitch dark we had to haul ourselves up it. Believe me, I found it a struggle, with my rifle slung on my shoulder with bayonet fixed and a shovel in one hand. When I reached the top there was a heap of dead. The ground was totally exposed to Turk fire. Two of the dead I recognised as our company sergeant-major and our company bugler. From that point it was just a matter of moving forward individually toward the entrenched Turks. We weren't in platoon or company formation. We were just individuals arriving by rope at the top of the cliff to meet Turkish fire. If you stayed where you were you got shot and if you advanced — which was the correct and proper thing to do — well, you still probably got shot, but you were at least advanced. The ground was steep and rugged and the vegetation was scrub, much of it native holly, six feet or more high; you simply had to push your way through it, finding your way individually, with heavy machine-gun fire coming in from the front and both flanks. It was impossible to see anything at all; it was quite hopeless. Just a matter of moving through bullets and meeting them, typical of events on Gallipoli. Hundreds of Otago men were lost in one or two hours. For myself, I was never, then or later, more in fear of losing my life; it seemed just a matter of when and where I stopped a bullet. I caught up with two Otago men from another platoon. One was a devout Roman Catholic named Dick. He was praying aloud to the Holy Mother Mary that he'd get hit, get a blighty wound that would see him off Gallipoli. He had his prayer answered quickly. He was hit and his friend was killed. My rifle was smashed in my hand in the same burst of Turkish fire. I thought at first that the tips of my fingers were blown off; it turned out just that bits of lead and zinc were imbedded in them. "I'm off now," Dick said. So far as I remember that was about the end of my part in events too. I can only tell you about that night from one individual's point of view. There is no other viewpoint possible. I never saw or got near a Turk that night. Nor perhaps did anyone else. Not a yard of ground was gained. The area became officially known as Deadman's Ridge.

Through that night and through the whole of the next day the

Otago Battalion drifted back to the beach in bits and pieces, ones and twos. It was perhaps two days before we could be assembled, and it was seen at last how few we were, as few as 200 of the 1000 landed on Gallipoli a week earlier. Ours was the first New Zealand battalion to be well and truly decimated. As we gathered again on the beach I may have been suffering from shock, but if I was, I have not relived it. Philosophical may be the word to describe my condition. What else could one be on Gallipoli?

What survived of our regiment was then shipped off down to Helles to help the British hold ground there. We were under the impression that we were to support British regulars of the 29th Division, but we were soon disillusioned in that respect. The 29th had taken large casualties by the time we arrived. After two or three days the New Zealanders were pushed toward impregnably entrenched Turks — the Auckland, Wellington and Canterbury regiments first. Because of our depletion the Otagos were left to last. But finally, as casualties grew, the Otagos were likewise ordered to advance in daylight across the patch of ground covered by intense Turkish fire which became known as the Daisy Patch. The remaining men of the Otago Battalion again took casualties. At the end of the day there were even fewer of the 200 survivors of May the second. We tried, as we had been trained, to cross the Daisy Patch in short rushes, by the whistle. But Turkish snipers, not to speak of machine-guns, proved themselves extremely effective at short range. Those of us who survived that fire finished up in an old Turkish trench and that was as far as we got. We were there two or three days until relieved by a very amateur lot of young and small British territorials in the middle of the night — a pig of a night, with rain lashing down. They were just boys, most of them, seventeen or eighteen years old, and physically most unimpressive compared to the Australians and New Zealanders on the peninsula. Their sergeant-major came along dumping these poor young chaps in our trench to hold it against the Turks. Relieved as we were to be getting out of that position, we couldn't help feeling sorry for them. Our commanding officer or perhaps junior officers or NCOs should have remained in the trenches to settle them in. These boys had seen no front-line action and were hopelessly up against it in that position. They were bound to suffer pretty fair casualties. I don't know what happened to them; that was the last we heard of that particular unit. To this day I remain sorry for those poor young fellows. We were marched back about eight miles to Cape Helles in the rain, and lay down soaking for the night in our billets among some olive trees. Eventually we were taken back to Anzac and again put into the line there. Cape Helles was a most unfortunate experience, and the crossing of the Daisy Patch a most unfortunate operation.

What all this meant to me personally, I suppose, is that I didn't take my boots off for the first three weeks of the Gallipoli campaign — from the landing on April the twenty-fifth, that is, through the attack on the second of May and my entire time at Cape Helles later in May. Aside from the fact that there was seldom an opportunity to remove my boots, my feet could get very cold at night. It was, of course, against all rules and regulations — even if I was a sergeant supposedly setting an example to my men. But there it was. When I did finally take my boots off it was in the front line, close to the Turks, at Quinn's Post. I slipped my boots off and wound puttees around my feet for warmth. Well, that night all hell broke loose — machine-guns and rifle fire — and we had to fall in. I had to struggle into my boots in the dark with all that happening. Meanwhile I lost my puttees. It was a great lesson. Afterwards, all my time at Anzac, I never took my boots off at night. There were of course other problems. I broke my dentures — my top plate — on an army biscuit. So then I had to manage these iron biscuits with only my bottom teeth. I used my entrenching tool to powder them as best I could.

I may have been afraid in positions such as Quinn's Post; I take it everyone was more or less afraid. Oddly, the thing that gave me greatest fear was not bullet or bomb but Turkish planes flying over and dropping metal darts down on us. They were about six inches long, very sharply pointed, and spun as they descended. I hated the thought of a dart dropping on my head. They seemed worse than bullets. You can't see bullets; they're past you even before you know they're coming. You could see shells arriving. You could see a four-inch shell coming over like a black cricket ball and you never knew exactly where it was going to land. You just hoped it was going to land somewhere you weren't. Big shells were best in that respect. What they called "whiz bang" shrapnel was more treacherous. You couldn't see it coming. It burst and either got you or missed you. We were never free of shrapnel and shell, or of casualties.

As for grief, there were too many lost friends to grieve for. The word "grief", in its literal sense, could not cover the range of one's feelings. I felt more sorrow for their mothers and fathers or sisters or wives, next of kin still suffering. The dead were no longer suffering. I took my feelings out on the vultures I saw flying over the battlefield. Not that I saw them feeding on dead bodies. But almost every morning twelve or fifteen of them would fly over the Anzac position toward the Turk lines. I had a shot at them every time they flew over. I never hit one, but I frightened them enough to make them fly off at a tangent. Otherwise I was quite fond of birds — I always have been a keen bird-watcher — but there were very few others to observe at Gallipoli. As for Turks, and killing them, the longer we were on Gallipoli, the less bitter front-line soldiers became toward them. We had our job and they had theirs. They had their ups and downs and casualties like us. They likewise had to live with decomposing dead, and the flies breeding among the dead, and swarming over us too, into our mouths and noses and eyes, making sleep impossible in the front line. We and the Turks were in exactly the same unfortunate position. Not that we felt sorry for them. If we'd felt sorry for them we'd have felt sorry for ourselves.

I was in charge of a sector in Courtney's Post when General Godley, the New Zealand commander, arrived for a visit. It was the only front-line inspection I saw him make. He had three or four high-ranking staff officers with him, but there was no mistaking General Godley. He wore his red tabs and stood six feet and three inches. He wasted no time in passing through; he seemed in a hurry to get back to the beach. It was a pretty poor performance, a lesson in how not to make such a visit to the front line. He never said, "Good day, boys" or "You're doing a good job here" or anything of the kind. He didn't even ask us a question, or look through a periscope at the Turk positions. He just went for his life through the trenches. I'm satisfied that he returned to headquarters, after visiting Courtney's Post, without having a clue as to what the ground between Courtney's and the Turks was like. I have often thought about it. Such people thought up the *modus operandi* of an attack on a Turkish position without knowing what the ground was like in our path. I should like to have seen what General Godley wrote in his diary that day. But who am I to say? I was only a ranker.

Misery was one of the disadvantages of Gallipoli, the smell of the dead, the flies, dysentery and food. One was not especially competent to survive Turkish shells, shrapnel and machine-guns, and naturally many did not. When I left the peninsula in July it was not because of a wound but simply because I was unable to walk any longer. It was sixty years before I landed there again, this time to walk the battlefield quite freely. The most menacing thing I saw was one small snake. I looked over the positions — like Quinn's and Courtney's — to which we had clung. I knew every yard of that ground; I knew the name of every Turkish height above us. I didn't need a guide. I don't imagine I have to explain why.

BILL

Bill East, talking lucidly in his Havelock North home in 1982, was perhaps the most powerful surviving New Zealand witness to the experience of Gallipoli. As a country boy, he was caught up in a campaign no one ever gave him time to understand. As a member of the Wellington Mounted Rifles, minus his horse, he saw out the greater part of the campaign, from May to August; and said goodbye to Gallipoli in the final, futile assault on Hill 60 — an especially lethal act of martial housekeeping, to make the British line look better in the stalemate after the August offensive. Telling his story he often shook with anguish. While protesting that he never wept, tears tracked down his cheeks. He felt as helpless and hurt in 1982 as he had in 1915.

I was working on a sheep farm near Taihape when war broke out. There were four of us farm-workers decided we'd join up. We were very much for the British Empire, being born in that groove. When the call came, we went. New Zealanders have got more sense now. They wouldn't ride off the way we did. Not on your life they wouldn't. We all got together in Taihape and went off to Palmerston North and joined up at the showgrounds there.

I had a black hunter horse, called Killarney, a beautiful beast. It was given to me by a farmer with a big estate. The first thing that happened was an officer coming along, and deciding he liked it. He took it and I was given a dud. The next blow was in Egypt. We had to give up our horses altogether and train as infantry in the desert. That was a terrible thing after being on horseback so long. So we became infantry and went ashore in May. We arrived in the middle of the night and couldn't see a thing. We really didn't know where we were. We hadn't been told anything.

General Godley finally turned up and told us to do our best for King and Country. That was about all. Otherwise all we could do was park ourselves safely, with the shells coming over, and build bivouacs — groundsheets laced together and propped up with sticks and biscuit tins. The biscuit tins were a mistake. They shone and drew Turkish fire. Eventually we took over trenches on Walker's Ridge.

We soon saw the landing was badly planned, and just a mess. We'd given the Turks a nod that we were coming. And we had no show whatever with the Turks dug in above us. All we could do was try and push them away. Hopeless. We were never told anything. No one gave us information. We just had to do as we were told. If they wanted us to attack we had to attack and that was it. We didn't know what it was for or anything else. They didn't tell us there was a machine-gun down in front of us which blew your head off if you didn't stay close to the ground. We'd be lucky to get back to the trenches, having accomplished nothing, and we'd sit wondering when the next attack was. We took stupid attacks as read. We weren't even angry. Everyone who was on that peninsula deserved a decoration, I don't care who it was. We were never safe anywhere. One night we were digging a sap quietly between trenches. We should have been safe. Our sergeant told us to take a rest. So we lay back on the soft dirt we dug. Then a ricochet bullet whined over and hit the sergeant as we lay there. It killed him. You didn't know where you were. One morning I woke in my bivvy and found a gaping hole. There was a spent bullet beside me. It had hit me in the behind, just leaving a big bruise.

Soon after we got to Gallipoli, while we were learning how to stay alive in the trenches, we had the biggest Turkish attack. We were ordered to stand to. We knew it was coming. A sergeant came alongside me. He said, "Come on, hold out your pannikin, where is it?" I found my pannikin, held it out, and he half-filled it with rum. But I didn't know what it was. I said to the joker next to me, "Here, what's this stuff?" He said, "Rum. Get it into you. It'll do you good." My parents were very religious. We never had alcohol in the house. I'd never tasted it. But I took a sip and coughed and spluttered and couldn't get my breath.

Then I made another attempt and swallowed the lot, and that was the end of me. I didn't know anything about the Turkish attack or anything else. I was flaked out at the bottom of the trench. All the shooting didn't wake me up. It was all over by eleven o'clock and I woke with the sun beaming down on me. I was too dopey even to lift my head and look through the loopholes at all the dead Turks lying in front of our trenches. That was my first fight.

Soon afterwards there was the armistice to clear the dead. I was mostly a spectator. Officers, ours and theirs, were talking to each other. Some blokes swapped cigarettes with the Turks. I didn't have anything to swap. The smell of the dead was dreadful, especially when you put bayonets into them. You had to bayonet the bodies to let all the gas out. Otherwise they were too swollen to be shifted. Our dead were dumped on blankets and dragged back to be buried on our side of the line. Most of the dead were Turks from their big attack. At the end of the armistice we got back into our trenches and started shooting at each other again.

I always had the feeling I was going to get home, so I wasn't so afraid. I was afraid up to a point, yes, but I tried to put it behind me. I believed there was a supreme being and that I was under his guiding hand. That was about as far as I could go. I couldn't pray; I didn't know how to any more. I'd had too much of that when I was young. But I saw one man afraid and I never want to see another one. He was a staff officer down at the bottom of Walker's Ridge. They couldn't get him out of his dugout. They did get him out one day, and he was a trembling wreck, the poor devil. He couldn't help it.

Early on we had to try and take number three outpost, out on our left, from the Turks. A bayonet charge is just a job like anything else. You hold your rifle with bayonet all fixed and go forward and if anything gets in your way you give it a jab. Then, when you're in a position to start firing, you fire. You can't just sit on your behind. You've got to do something. What I remember of that lot is getting right under a Turkish trench. A Turk came up in front of me and I just swung my rifle round with bayonet fixed. I caught him somewhere because he dropped. Then it was all retreat, trying to make our own way back, with the wounded too, those we could drag with us. The Turks spreadeagled the body of our sergeant, who got killed in the attack, out over the front of their trench. We were disgusted to think they could do such a thing.

Otherwise things could get boring. We just looked through periscopes, over the top, and wandered round and waited for orders and had a bit of a doze when we could. Just filling in time, that's all. And surviving. Surviving was pure luck. Death came along pretty regularly. You'd hear someone had been killed, someone wounded, and you couldn't take it too much to heart. You just said, "Poor devil" and got on with your day.

I was taken off the peninsula with dysentery before the big August fight. I was running all the time. I couldn't enjoy my food. We were down to skin and bone. Dysentery just ate away our intestines.

When I got back in September there were a lot of faces missing. My mate, Clutha McKenzie, whom I joined up with, was gone. He'd been blinded by British naval shells dropping short on Chunuk Bair. He'd collected the blast and lost his eyes. The ones left after that August fight were pretty dejected. They'd been in the fight for some time and it takes a long time to get over what they'd been through. Especially with the tucker we'd been getting. There was never enough food to build you up again. Just enough to survive on, that's all.

So we had this attack on Hill 60. I was a rake-in for that one. We all were. The left-overs. You just had to do what you were told and follow the leader. The men lined up for the attack were all fairly disgruntled and dejected. They'd just about had it. We were only told we were attacking the Turk trenches ahead and we would be given the signal to charge. Not what the attack was for, or anything else. So we lay there waiting with our bayonets fixed. When the word came, our major, Major Bruiser Taylor, was right in front of me as he jumped to his feet. He had a sword he wasn't supposed to have — because of swords drawing Turk fire — and he blew his whistle and pulled his sword out and shouted "Charge!" That's all he said. The next thing he was flat on his face, shot through the head. I didn't know whether to go back or forward and I decided to go forward and all the rest were coming with me across an open piece of ground. We were just anyone's mutton. We managed to finish up in a Turk trench and lined up again, shooting toward the Turks as hard as we could. I was next to a Canterbury Mounted man who'd been in the battle for Chunuk Bair in August. I said to him, "What sort of an outfit is this?" He said, "Not nearly as bad as Chunuk Bair." I said, "It's bad enough." Next thing we knew there was enfilade fire down our trench from the big .75 guns to our right. I don't know what happened to the Canterbury man — he's probably still over there on Hill 60 — but I got sprayed with pellets in the blast. I got them in the lung. I had to drag myself away, feeling weaker all the time. That was all I could do. Get out of it. Otherwise I was in everyone's way.

I never cried, but it was the only time I ever felt like crying, that day. As I crawled away from Hill 60 I met three or four of our fellows wounded, badly wounded, dying, singing out for water. I threw them my water bottle. There were four of them. Badly wounded. Suffering. And I couldn't do anything. But I threw them my water bottle. It was all I could do, all I could give them. My water bottle. That was why I was almost crying. Was Gallipoli worth it, worth all that suffering?

After that lot I was dug in down at Anzac Cove, on a stretcher. The only man who spoke to me was old Padre Grant. He saw that I was put on a ship. Then he went back to our unit and got killed.

That was how I finished on Gallipoli. Carried off. I looked back and saw a hash. A waste of time and lives. I put in four and a half years of my life, altogether, in the First World War. For nothing. Nothing. You wonder whether it's worthwhile or not fighting for freedom. There's no freedom when nobody's got a say in anything. Everybody's got a lot to say but nobody takes any notice. I wouldn't advise anyone to go to war again. Not the way we rode off to it in 1914. I wouldn't want anyone to go through what we went through. What is war for? We could have done with some information on that too.

JOE

Ex-schoolmaster Joe Gasparich — small, gnomic, often pedantic on points of detail — was found in a home for the elderly in Napier in 1982. He sat up jauntily in a wheelchair as he told his tale. The most eloquent of veterans interviewed, never lacking in vocabulary, Joe survived the first days of the campaign, and afterwards the last, as a sergeant in the Auckland Infantry Battalion.

When the war began in 1914 I was teaching in a school at Whangarei, and hating it. I volunteered immediately because I knew all my mates would. My mates were all rugby men. So in we got — and the whole lot of us went together. There was a sense of adventure about it all, yes, but I don't think you could have found a more patriotic volunteer than myself. I loved old England and everything that England had done. Where others criticised, I found excuses for her. I gloried in Britain, the British people, and the British Empire. New Zealand's being part of the British Empire meant a great deal to me. It had to mean a great deal if one was to confront a virile and active enemy, armed with modern weapons, as we did on the first day of the landing.

I arrived in Anzac Cove, one of the earliest New Zealanders ashore, as one of the thirty men selected to form General Godley's guard. I was rather surprised at the barrenness of the place as the boats finally grounded. It was a plain sandy beach, with the land lifting immediately beyond. Otherwise there was nothing specially to distinguish the location but for a dead body directly in our path. He was an able seaman from one of the British vessels involved in the landing. I caught my breath a bit. He was the first dead man I'd ever seen. Bullets were flying around, of course, and shrapnel. We didn't have time to think much about anything.

The men ahead were scaling those sudden hills, and meeting up with the Turk, or Jacko as we called him. I don't think we had butterflies as they were commonly called. I was more exhilarated than fearful. We'd arrived. This was what we'd been aiming at ever since we'd joined the show. We were meeting the enemy for the first time in real war. Looking for trouble, that is, and meeting it. But on that first day my job was no more than manhandling and dispatching boxes of ammunition to the front line.

Soon after the landing the losses in the Auckland Regiment were such that half General Godley's guard, me included, were recalled to their platoons to make up the numbers. We were moved down to Helles to help the British establish their hold at that end of the peninsula. The Daisy Patch, as it became known, is very vividly impressed on my memory. For many of us it was the most bitter event of all. It suggested how things were to be.

Our first night at Helles was spent in vacated British trenches. There was a Turkish hand protruding from one of the trenches, with an opal ring on a fat finger. There wasn't much else to consider. Why we were there no one knew. The next day, in what has become known as the second battle for Krithia, I was moving forward to the left all day under fire, taking thirty men with me, not knowing where we were going, across a big open grassy area. We had a large number of casualties. "Where are we going?" men asked. "Follow me," was all I could tell them.

The point is that here I was, a sergeant, in charge of a lot of these fellows, and I didn't know what the objective was. There was this hill in the distance, Achi Baba, quite a mound, and we knew the general idea was to capture that. Otherwise we were never told where the enemy was, or what we were supposed to do. We were greenhorns in this war, in any war, and had nothing but guts going for us. The marvellous thing was that we stuck at it. I tried to link up with a lieutenant named Macfarlane; he was supposed to be establishing a front line. We battled through low scrub and found some Aucklanders whom we presumed to be in the front line. "Macfarlane's out there," I was told. "Hear the firing?" We could hear the firing all right. That was our direction. I pushed men across in short rushes and lost quite a number. We arrived on a ridge capped by several pines, where three or four Aucklanders were sheltering, including my platoon commander. Like me he was looking for the front line, not finding it, and losing men along the way. He started talking to me and then collapsed, shot dead. "Have you got some water?" one fellow asked me. "My water bottle's been shot through." I went to offer him some and found my water bottle had been shot through too. That was what the fire was like. We still couldn't see a sign of a Turk anywhere. Here we were, then, in this scrubby country, with more and more men falling, and not a Turk in sight; we weren't even sure of which direction to shoot in. What could we do? No enemy and yet men dropping all the time. "It's no good mucking around here," I argued. "Let's look somewhere else." So I gathered up the few men still fit and alive and tried to advance, further still to the left, moving out into the more open terrain which was soon to become notorious as the Daisy Patch. Grassy and shrubby, it was, and patched everywhere brightly by daisies. We were told to dig in. Each fellow, with his outdated entrenching tool, dug a hole into which he could squeeze himself and make himself feel safer. The idea was that the holes would eventually merge into a single trench. For a start we could only lie on our bellies and scratch. Every time we threw up earth we drew a shower of bullets. Now and then I crawled off with my rifle and fired off a shot at where I thought the Turks might be. What we didn't yet comprehend was that Jacko was dug in well above us, looking down on everything we did. Throwing up earth made us perfect targets. It was dreadfully hot. I stuck my bayonet in the wall of my hole as a clothes peg and hung my tunic and webbing on it. Then the word came along that the whole front was to advance at five thirty. That order was our first indication that we were actually in the front line.

No sooner was the word given than a mob of Aucklanders jumped up to my right and yelled their heads off. "Come on, you bastards," they called. "Give them hell." They hadn't understood the order; they didn't know the time. Isolated in our holes, none of us knew the time. Watches were all awry; they hadn't been checked. And here were these men scampering across open ground and calling out to us to follow. What were we to do? When I went away I made a vow to myself that if ever we were going to rush an enemy in open country I was going to go over in the first wave. Whoever the enemy was he would not be expecting the first wave. The second, yes. Which is exactly how it went. Anxious not to be left behind, and to catch that first wave, I hopped up, pulled on my tunic and webbing, grabbed my rifle and bayonet, and ran. By the time I took off these fellows were a hundred yards ahead and halfway across the Daisy Patch. Bullets were whizzing all around but none of them touched me. There were fellows lying very still, and others wounded and waving their hands for attention. I caught up with the survivors lined up in a dry watercourse. At last, after all this time, we could see Jacko ahead, and what we saw stunned us — there Jacko was, entrenched right along the ridge ahead, perhaps a hundred yards away. He was underground, timber and sandbags and sods overhead, and safe as houses. He could see and shoot through apertures without any risk from return fire. And we had to attack that! We were stonkered. It was impossible, madness, to try to take that Turk ground. I tried to get shots in. I complained to the fellow on my right that the banging of his rifle close to my ear was upsetting my aim. And while we were firing at this forbidding position ahead, blow me down if a Turkish officer didn't rise up from it, standing on the roof, waving a sword. Perhaps he was overexcited, or trying to wing his way to heaven faster. It was too much for me. I thought that if he could stand up and flourish a sword, of all things, I could stand up and shoot him. I rose, took a steady bead on the gentleman, squeezed the trigger, and to this day don't know what happened. Because then I got a whale of a bang on the elbow, and I thought it was this fellow who had been irritating me. My rifle dropped to the ground, and I grabbed my arm, and my hand felt hot. I looked down and there was blood squirting out of my arm. I had been smacked twice. I slithered down into a little gully, dropping my rifle, out of the fight altogether. One of the boys ripped off my sleeve and roughly bandaged me up.

So, there we were, those of the first wave, pinned down and marooned. I looked back and saw the utterly senseless attack launched across the Daisy Patch become even more appalling. More and more New Zealanders were ordered to follow us. I saw a couple of groups start to make the formal attack and some came on and dropped, and a third group came on and everyone dropped, and a fourth started off and four or five dropped and the rest finally turned and hopped back into their holes. I thought, well, at least that lot have sense; they have saved their lives. They were expected to make zig-zag dashes across a wholly open area exposed to enemy rifle and machine-gun. Yet again I watched every single man in one party fall as he was hit so that none reached the spot where we had shallow cover. The grassy daisy-covered space soon became a pathetic field of dead. Other lines followed and, except for those men who swiftly returned to cover, the same fate awaited all who tried to reach us. Just one wounded man staggered across to us and fell. I was aghast at the utterly wanton waste of valuable lives.

I found myself sitting useless alongside Captain Bartlett, second in command of the 15th North Auckland Company. He was wounded too. I said to him, "Sir, this is a sheer waste of good men. I'm going back. I'm going to risk going back to see if I can stop this madness." He didn't argue with me. So I took off my webbing, stripped down to my tunic, and leaving my rifle behind, set off at a gallop back across the Daisy Patch. The dead were lying everywhere, little silent bundles of New Zealanders. Instead of heading straight across, as I had before, I took a slant to the left. The ground was jumping and the bushes were swaying this way and that, and it sounded as if I were running through a giant swarm of bees on the move. They weren't bees. They were bullets buzzing around my ears, everywhere. The landscape was alive with bullets. Nothing touched me. Then I fell into a sap some Pommies were digging, about three feet deep. I plonked in among them, my blood spilling all over the place. I was bone dry and needed a drink but they didn't have water, just their rum ration. I took a good swig of that, and that just about finished me. That, and getting my wounds doused with iodine. Of course my dash back to the rear accomplished nothing. By the time I tried to report my feelings from the front line about that useless attack it was too late. The bloodied Daisy Patch itself, strewn with New Zealand men, so many of whom I knew, had its own message. We blamed the system, of course. The system that sent men out to fight without telling them what they were fighting for, what our objective was. I was a sergeant pushing men at an enemy, and yet knowing nothing myself.

Eventually I was taken to England in a hospital ship, and returned to Gallipoli after the August offensive. At Anzac there had not been a great improvement. The Turk was still up the top, with the advantage of looking down all the time, seeing what we were doing, and acting accordingly. We were always hopelessly up against it. All we could do was entrench at night and put out patrols when we could, and bleed away, from bullets and dysentery, among hundreds of decomposing dead. Most of the time I was on Rhododendron Ridge, from which the failed assault on Chunuk Bair had been mounted in August, and the dead were only too visible. Sometimes we crawled out at night, little groups of us, to try and bring our own dead back in. But there were too many of them for us to make much impression. And finally we were as helpless against the flies as we were against the Turk. They bred in millions among the swollen, rotten bodies scattered in the scrub. From this oozing matter where they bred so promiscuously they would move to the open latrines and then to the living. They sought moisture from our ears, our noses, our eyes, our mouths. We wrapped our heads in hessian in an endeavour to escape them until we were nearly suffocated by the heat and still the flies managed to get at us. If you spilled a drop of water in a trench the flies would suddenly be seething in four or five deep on that spot, frantic for moisture. You had to keep a moving hand over any morsel of food or drink in a forlorn attempt to keep the flies from entering your mouth. As we dug trenches, or tried to sleep, the flies swarmed on our faces.

Then there was the dysentery. It attacked the abdomen and lower bowel until, in some cases, the torn inside of the colon protruded from the anus. I was soon passing slime and blood. I felt as if my whole alimentary tract was on fire. I saw fellows literally dying on the latrines. They crawled to the latrines — they couldn't find anyone fit enough to carry them — and they died on the latrines. They were then buried anywhere about. And yet blokes survived. I survived that. I was taken off the peninsula to Imbros where I was housed in a large marquee with dozens of other fellows in like state. We slept on the ground and were fed stew and tea which just made matters worse. Visits to the latrines were an agony. More men died there. There were long queues for latrines in the boats which took us back to Egypt, and there the squatting toilets in a Cairo hospital were a final refinement in our torture.

I got back to the peninsula for the last of the campaign, with the weather turning cooler. I was again on Rhododendron Spur, under the Turks on Chunuk Bair, and it wasn't a bad place. It was solid and you could keep down under cover and get warm when the frost and snow came, the rain too. We wore greatcoats for warmth when we went on trench duty. Once my greatcoat was first soaked, then frozen stiff, while I was on duty. When I finished my spell I left it outside my dugout. It stood sentinel there for several days before it thawed out. That was how cold it was. And we lived lousy as bandicoots, warmed underground by the polluted air of our own bodies.

When we heard evacuation of the peninsula was being contemplated, though, we simply could not believe it. It took a long, long time to convince us that it was really being considered by the high command. We could not understand two things. One was withdrawing in the face of an enemy. The second was leaving our cobbers behind, those buried on the peninsula. You cannot imagine how that hurt us. Only someone who was actually there could understand our feelings. We had gone through so much together, the living and the dead. We belonged together. We would rather hang on than leave them, no matter how hopeless the situation.

But it was true. The evacuation did come. We did have to leave our cobbers behind. I volunteered for the rearguard. Fewer and fewer men were left manning the trenches as others were smuggled off the peninsula at night. If the Turks guessed what was going on, and launched an attack, we few would have to try fighting them off while others made good their escape. I was one of the last men to leave our position on Rhododendron Spur in the silent night evacuation. It was 2.30 in the morning and everything was so absolutely, eerily empty. The trenches were solid with ice, and I could hear the sound of my boots echoing right down the trench, down the gully, running ahead of me. Talk about empty! I was alone at last, for the first time in the war, absolutely alone; it was quite weird. I heard a rather unnerving wail from the Turk trenches at one stage, which suggested an imminent attack — at least in my nervous and solitary state. I didn't see a soul until I finally made my rendezvous with the chap in charge of the evacuation. Soon after that it was all over. We were all off, still grieving for those we left behind.

Looking back, of course I see war as a waste of men and of time. It didn't settle anything. Even the First World War hasn't been settled yet, has it? What did we win? What did we get? But Gallipoli made me more proud of being a New Zealander. My company was made up of bushmen, timber workers and gumdiggers from Northland. They lived hard, hard lives, and could be trusted with anything. They had commanded my respect in peace; they confirmed that respect in adversity. The shaping of the New Zealand character had been going on a long time, but you could say that Gallipoli, terrible though it was, consolidated the character of the New Zealander. It made us grow up — if you can understand the idea behind the thought of growing up. We lost our innocence all right. I think that is true. I would think so.

VIC

Eighty-eight-year-old Vic Nicholson, with his wife his most attentive and awed listener, talked in his modest Palmerston North home in 1983. He saw Gallipoli out as a member of the doomed and decimated Wellington Infantry Battalion. Vic was nevertheless forthcoming, though he was, as it turned out, confiding his experience of Gallipoli, and especially of his hours on Chunuk Bair, for the first time. The gaps in his narrative were not due to failure of memory. Recall became too painful, and, at times, too tearful for him to continue. It seemed Vic had been on Chunuk Bair for most of a century, with never a living soul in sight.

I was working out an engineering apprenticeship in Gisborne when the war began. Joining up was the thing to do at the time. Three of my best friends joined and I made it four. It was more high adventure than anything else. Mind you, I felt patriotic about the British Empire too. I was fond of war stories and Empire stories. We were worried because the war might be over before we got there. That it was only going to last a few weeks. We couldn't get there fast enough, to be in the show. Egypt, when we landed there, was all hard training. We were subjected to pretty severe route marches up to twenty-four miles a day, with a full pack on and the top screwed onto your water bottle, which was where it was supposed to stay. I think that hard training in Egypt was responsible for a lot of the sickness we had on the Gallipoli peninsula. Men grew restless. They started to say, "What the hell are we here for?" Even on the dawn of the move to the Dardanelles we didn't know where we were going. We were just going. We had more reliable information from a fortune-teller we met in Egypt. Three of us were coming out of Shepherd's

Hotel at Cairo one night. We were waylaid by an old scallywag who offered to tell our fortune for two piastres or some other fine sum. We had just enough supercargo to say, "Righto, mate, away you go." I was first through. He said, "You are going to fight in a war, and you will be wounded but not killed. You will go home." Then he went through the other chaps. He said to the next, "You will be in a fight too, but I don't know about you." To the third of us he said, "You will be mixed up in the same fight and injured, badly injured, but you will go home." The fortune-teller said quickly, "I don't know any more" and took off. But that was how things turned out. I was wounded and got home. The second man was killed on Chunuk Bair. The third survived with shell shock, and never really recovered from it, though he lived on many more years.

I didn't go ashore on Gallipoli until April the twenty-seventh. When we were on the island of Lemnos, before the invasion fleet sailed, an officer told us, "Now there's some of you blokes going to be left behind to clean up and so you can't all go. We're not going to call for volunteers because we know we won't get any. So we're going to put names into a hat." My name came out of the hat. It was like a kick in the teeth. So I had to stay back on Lemnos cleaning up while everyone else sailed on to Gallipoli. There were about 250 of us tidying up the mess tens of thousands of troops had left. On April the twenty-seventh, two days after the landing, we were taken to Gallipoli on a British destroyer. We knew we were in a war within a mile of Anzac Cove. Bargeloads of wounded were being ferried out past us. We started to lose men right away to shot and shell. We lost between twelve and fifteen men as we were finally rowed ashore. Some recovered. Some didn't. It was the one time I felt I perhaps shouldn't be there, that I might have been a bit too ambitious. War was pretty severely thrust upon you as you arrived in Anzac Cove. The men I went ashore with were mostly Australians, and I found myself in the Fourth Battalion of the Australian Infantry. It took me three days, in all the confusion and commotion, to find my own unit. They were in the front line up Walker's Ridge. When I arrived I found that five out of my eight tent-mates had disappeared. I'd ask, "Where's old Nick, where's he gone?" I'd get the answer, "We haven't seen him since the landing, so God knows where he is." Nobody seemed able to tell you how they died.

A lot of Wellington's time was eventually to be spent at Quinn's Post. It was really a fort. It gradually developed from an open trenchline into a fortification with sealed-in trenches and overhead protection, the whole lot. We had wire-netting up to stop bombs thrown from the Turk line. If they hit the wire, they rolled back down the parapet into no-man's-land and exploded there. If they went over the top of the netting they rolled down a hill to our rear. Quinn's was absolutely isolated, out on a little peninsula, as it were, from the Anzac sector. Turk guns were trained on it from all directions. One day I saw a movement across the ground up toward Pope's and I fired at it. Half a minute later I got a whiz bang shell back at me. That was a nasty moment. I had a worse one later on when I was on watch, about two o'clock in the morning. There was only about thirty-five feet of no-man's-land between us and the Turk trenches. I thought I saw movement out there. Lofty Chapman, my tent-mate, was asleep beside me. I gave Lofty a kick, and I said, "Have a look at this, I think there's movement out front." He said, "Bugger you. I'm having a good sleep." So I went on with my watch and again I thought I saw movement. I kicked Lofty again and told him. He got up in a bad mood. I moved off the firestep and Lofty moved up. He clapped his eye to the loophole and was shot right through the eye. That was the last of my tent-mate Lofty. I didn't cry, unless Gallipoli was one long cry. If you cried once you'd never stop. There were friends going every day and sometimes every hour of the day, wonderful friends. I grieved inwardly. That was all you could do. As a war went on you could forget the death of a very fine friend in five minutes. My sorrow, so far as Gallipoli is concerned, is all those mates I lost. That, and never having a decent look at the place.

At Quinn's you could never put your head up and have a good look. If some enterprising boy hadn't adapted a few old rifles, and made them periscopic, there would have been even more casualties. They were crude but they were wonderful. They helped us hold Quinn's. They should be in every military museum in the world. The most terrible thing at Quinn's was the stench of the dead. The bodies were only yards away. There was no relief from that brain-numbing stench. Otherwise we were good landlords. We were proud of keeping the place tidy. We'd warn other units, when they came in to relieve us for a while, "You look after the place, and leave it as you found it." Quinn's to all intents and purposes belonged to the Wellington Infantry Battalion, and we were very proud and proprietorial. Then there was the tunnelling. It was a silly old business, but frightening. We'd tunnel toward the Turk trenches and they'd tunnel toward us. And place charges. It was always night working down in the tunnels. You'd be pushed along one of these tunnels toward the working face and there you'd chip away with your little entrenching tool, and scrape the soil into a sandbag and pass it on down a line of blokes until it was disposed of. It was even more frightening when you listened and heard a Turk tapping away somewhere underground nearby too. I don't think our main charge in the mine gallery under Quinn's was ever blown. I don't think anyone was game. I think it would have blown everyone, the Turks and us too, through the roof.

Boredom was something you had to fight too. Through June and July, up to the big offensive in August, the boredom was draining. There was nothing to do and nowhere to go to avoid it in a place like Quinn's. You'd look for someone you knew to talk to, like someone who'd been off wounded and had got back again. They might have seen a girl, a woman who was good to look at, while they were in hospital. They'd talk about her. Little things from another world. If you were back on the beach for a break you'd go and look for the Indians and cadge a chapati off them. Food was everything. At no time on Gallipoli was the food reasonable or fit to eat. Even the water ferried ashore through the breakers was brackish and foul. As for food, the tins of bully beef stood in hot sun, in probably 100 or 115 degrees fahrenheit of heat for days and days and days. It was just cat's meat floating around in a tin of oil. That was your lot. Try making a hearty meal out of that.

We knew the August attack was coming for a long time. The big sap we were digging out to the left of the Anzac position,

in all our fatigue time, wasn't for drainage purposes. What we
didn't anticipate was that we were going to be pushed up into
the high country, into the Sari Bair range, rather than across the
flats in from Suvla Bay. We didn't know we were going high
until we congregated at the end of the big sap on a day in August.
Then we were told what we were supposed to do. So up we went.
We moved at dusk. There were one or two skirmishes on the way.
The object of the exercise was total silence. No bullets. Only the
bayonet. But we heard this haka and war cries from the Maoris
when they hit the Turks. There wasn't a man left when the Maoris
had finished with them. We were instructed at all times to
maintain the line of advance. In that steep terrain it was an
impossibility. We became little groups sticking at it until we could
find a way up and through. In places the line was just one or
two persons. It was very erratic until we got up to the Apex, short
of Chunuk Bair. Then we got into some sort of order for the
main advance.

That was early in the morning of August the eighth. I was very
near the right of the line. The first I knew of the fighting was
rifle fire to my left as we got to the top. Chunuk Bair was only
a ridge, and it was well covered by the Turks on Hill Q and by
others on high ground. The first we knew was rifle fire and a
bayonet attack. When we got to the top we didn't have time to
look at the view. I never saw the Narrows. There were just hills
and more hills and we asked ourselves, "Where do we go from
here?" Because there didn't seem anywhere to go. At that stage
we didn't know where we were. We were told later that Hill 971
was our objective, some 1400 yards on. Who knows? Nobody
thought to mention it. There we were on Chunuk Bair.

We were soon getting even less of a view. The rifle fire became
more and more intense until there was just a sheet of bullets,
almost at ground level. Our field of fire was between us and Turk
heads coming up over the hill. The first thing we saw of them
was heads. Heads were our targets. There soon seemed to be
thousands of them. The heads, our targets, got bigger as they
came closer. By the time the Turks were fully in view they were
within twenty feet, in bayonet range. It was time to start with
the bayonet. Then you discovered that your rifle was too hot to

hold. I mean red hot, practically on fire. You had to grab for a cold one, perhaps a Turkish rifle. As long as it was cold. As the attacks became more intense Wellington infantrymen had two or three rifles, one to shoot from and the others to use for bayoneting. Short rifles and short bayonets were best. The bayonet fighting seemed to last weeks; I suppose it was only minutes. No one likes bayonets, and the Turks seemed to like them even less than us. I don't remember any charges. It was all stand and defend with the bayonet, just a mad whirl. In the back of my head I could hear the words, "Get the bastard before he gets you. Get him or he'll get you!" That was the fact of the matter. I don't remember bayonets going in. Perhaps I shut my eyes. I don't know who I killed and who I didn't. There's always the chance that people with very bad wounds will recover. So you don't know. I wasn't conscious of all the fighting around on Chunuk Bair. Only that in my little area. At one point eight or nine of us were cut off and surrounded by Turks. They motioned for us to put our rifles down and hands up. But we got stuck in and got out. It was they who finally had their hands in the air. That episode seemed to last hours, but it must have been a fraction of a minute. The Turks were heaving bombs at us too. We had no bombs, and we couldn't shoot back at bombs. And it was hot, hard and thirsty. It's only when your tongue actually rattles round in your mouth that you can say you are thirsty. That's no fable. Actually rattling round in your mouth. We stripped off our tunics and we were fighting in singlets and in the buff. No one had hats or badges or identification. The Turks were the same. Soon it was so you could only identify a Turk by his hat, his whiskers and swarthy complexion.

I lost my dearest friend, Teddy Charles, that day. We joined up together and saw the campaign through together until Chunuk Bair. There were no officers left, no NCOs. Just soldiers. Teddy led thirty men forward to try and hold the ridge. He called, "Come on, Vic," but I was impeded by Turkish fire. We never saw those thirty men again. Later, in the dark, I thought I heard Teddy's voice calling for his mother, then for me. By then the place was crawling with Turks and I couldn't get to him. He's still on Chunuk Bair, a pile of bones.

We were terribly aware of our wounded as the day went on. They filled our little forward trench. It was only three feet deep in the first place. It wasn't long before the dead and wounded were so piled in the trench that we were trampling on them, standing on them, with cover only up to our knees. All the time you were thinking, "What can we do for them?" But there wasn't anything. There wasn't anything you could for them. They might have been friends but there was nothing to be done. It would have been suicide for a stretcher-bearer to come forward to us. There was just this curtain of fire across the crest of Chunuk Bair, a foot to eighteen inches above the earth. I know stories that we shot some of our own wounded up there, on Chunuk Bair. Personally I never had to face up to that one. And yet, no doubt, it would have been a mercy, a blessing, for wounded to have been shot by their own men. The bombs that went into the trench made even more carnage among the wounded and dying underfoot. There were more and more dead. If I was asked to give a description of the colour of the earth on Chunuk Bair on the eighth or ninth of August, I would say it was a dull or browny red. And that was blood. Just blood.

It seems Otago blokes decided that Wellingtons up the front were getting it pretty hot. They fixed their bayonets and came up and mingled with the Wellingtons in our sector and gave us a hand. At least I have that impression. It might have been another Angel of Mons. An illusion. A vision. That's what things were like. The pressure seemed to ease. You didn't seem so lonely. But the crowd on the other side didn't diminish much. I saw our Colonel Malone occasionally that day. He was moving about a fair amount. He kept boosting our morale, and he always had a kind word, an encouraging word. "It'll ease off shortly," he promised. "They'll get tired of this." Little nothings. Then he suddenly went missing and we heard he had been killed marking out a trench line. Many of our wounded were never seen again. They would slide down to the bottom of ravines, not be able to get out, and die there. We had to empty the dead from our trenches and drop them into the ravines too. Their bones are still there. I was on Chunuk Bair until the ninth of August. No food, no water, and the Turks were as safe as churches until they were

in yards of our bayonets. In a lull in the fighting I would go and
collect water bottles from our dead. You had to keep yourself
going. No one else could. British troops relieved us on the ninth
and were hit by enfilade fire from their own men. Gurkhas
climbing Hill Q were wiped out by shellfire from a British
destroyer. I remember moving downhill in the dark. There was
a bloke screaming somewhere, screaming terribly. He could have
been a New Zealander. He could have been a Turk. We looked
for him in the dark and never found him. He just went on
screaming.

Scared? Sometimes you were too scared to be scared. I would
laugh at any individual who says he wasn't afraid. Those who
say they are devoid of fear talk absolute phooey. I was paralysed
with fear. I was so paralysed with fear on Chunuk Bair and in
other places on Gallipoli that I was sometimes incapable of action,
but lucky enough to get away. Strange to say, though, at no point
did I ever think that I wouldn't get home. I was wounded but
I did get home. I was torpedoed in the *Triumph* but I still got
home. That fortune-teller in Cairo had it right.

I was wounded, after we'd lost the summit, on August the
fifteenth. I was out with a party covering engineers laying barbed
wire and hit through the shoulder. I walked to a dressing station
where the wound was plugged. I was given half a pannikin of
rum and told to make my own way back to the beach. I met
a man who had half a leg blown away. We helped each other
down. I don't know how we made it. Perhaps the rum floated
us down. I left Gallipoli two days later. The Gallipoli campaign
was very little use to anybody. We never got further than 2000
yards into Turkey and took months and thousands of dead to
do it. The orders were so mad that you wondered whether you
were mad or the lunatic who gave the orders. It was noticeable
that the author of the campaign, Winston Churchill, never showed
his face in Australia or New Zealand. World War I and World
War II were supposed to be for the good of civilisation. The good
hasn't come off. Havoc and sorrow and distress don't make a
good foundation for a better world, for anything at all. The fact
is that New Zealanders were led up the garden path. No one
wanted to admit it then or later. I have waited seventy years for

the truth to be told about it, which it's never been, and if I live to see the day perhaps I will die less angry.

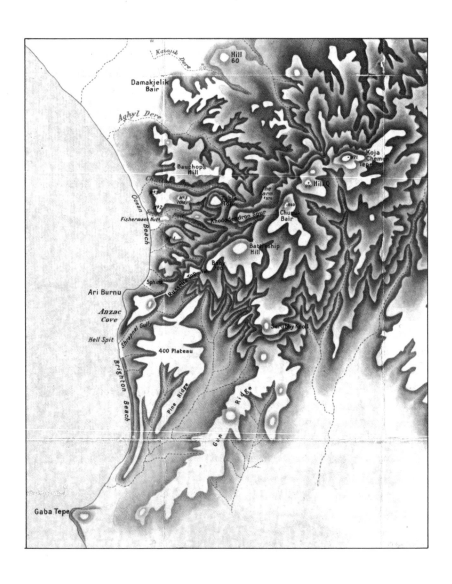

The Campaign

Most nations have days to celebrate wars of liberation and triumphant feats of arms. New Zealand does not. Anzac Day, 25 April, began as an anniversary of a national disaster, one which gutted a young country of its bravest and brightest. It was a never less than anguished campaign in which nearly 3,000 New Zealanders were cut down; a campaign which heralded the death of many thousands more in the trenches of France. For most of the world they perished in a futile battle best forgotten — a sickening sideshow of World War I which is remembered, where recalled elsewhere at all, under the name Gallipoli. For many New Zealanders, though, Gallipoli has remained as potent a placename as any in the outside world, a name as familiar as Taupo or Timaru, but one which chills the heart.

The Gallipoli campaign — as New Zealanders knew it — had its beginnings in Victorian and Edwardian decades. New Zealand began the twentieth century as a frontier society. Cities were small, factories few. We remained most conspicuously a rural people, still felling forest, founding farms, shifting hills for roads and bridging rivers for railways, establishing a new society in a long untamed land. Our largest ambition was to make New Zealand a vast farm to feed Britain. From the last decades of the twentieth century that ambition now seems remarkably remote, touchingly innocent.

We weren't yet proud of ourselves as New Zealanders, as a people with distinct identity, perhaps a distinct destiny, in the world. We were proud of our advanced social legislation. We had begun to be proud of our brawny rugby players. But our largest pride was in being British. Novelist Anthony Trollope had already summed us up in the 1870s: 'The New Zealander among

97

John Bulls is the most John Bullish. He admits the supremacy of England to every other place in the world, only he is more English than the Englishman at home. New Zealand considers herself the cream of the British Empire.'

The *New Zealand School Journal* told young New Zealanders: 'The Empire looks to you in time of need, to think, to labour and to bear hardships on its behalf...' The editor of the *New Zealand Herald* could speak in this way: 'We were never a military nation, always a naval nation. We relied upon our fleets to guard us for four hundred years.' We? New Zealand? A naval nation? Of course not. The editor had no concept of New Zealand as other than an offshore appendage of Britain. 'We' meant the British Empire. Typical of most public figures was Truby King, the celebrated founder of the Plunket Society. He told New Zealand's women that their role in the world was to breed bigger and better babies for the British Empire.

Without a clear notion of our own identity, indeed of our own location in the world, we were mystically devoted to the Empire, to British monarchs who took that devotion so much for granted that they never voyaged out to their distant colony. Australia might be crammed with dissident Irishmen with small respect for the British Crown; New Zealanders, aside from a muttering minority of radicals, were loyal. That loyalty had already led us into one war which was not, on the face of things, any of our business at all. To keep the Empire in business, and the world's maps coloured with Britannic red, 6000 New Zealanders volunteered to fight South Africa's Boers between 1899 and 1902. Indeed we were offering our soldiers two weeks before war was declared; and they were on their way little more than a week after fighting began. This ugly colonial war remained terra incognita to flag-waving New Zealanders at home. The fact was, however, that many New Zealanders at the front of the fray found more in common with rebellious Boer colonists than with their British commanders. Always more independent and impatient with martial injustice than imperial troops, New Zealanders even called a strike or two against their own officers. The official view, however, was that the war was 'a glorious page in our history... The whole nation is aroused, and the Imperial spirit has taken a firm hold.'

Or so it certainly seemed. Our young had been sent away with imperial songs, and welcomed home as heroes of the Empire. Only sixty died in action; far more succumbed to enteric fever. Nevertheless New Zealand's attitude to war was determined. No alien bayonets would bristle on our shore. Others would involve us in wars in far places, lands of which we knew next to nothing. And war's more shocking truths would remain remote. We would sing young men off, and cheer them home, with no real notion of what personal hells they had survived — or even of quite what they had been up to. It might fairly be supposed that we didn't want to know; we wanted no flaws in the imperial fabric.

New Zealand's politicians, who found votes in beating the Empire's drum, were at pains to prove that we were ready and willing to fight Britain's wars. We contributed a dreadnought to Britain's navy. We welcomed Field Marshal Lord Kitchener, Britain's most conspicuous soldier, with devout cheers. From 1909 all male New Zealanders between the ages of fourteen and thirty were compulsorily trained as part-time territorial soldiers. Objectors were jailed. Even Britain herself did not have such ruthless and wide-ranging conscription. We imported a reliable Briton, Major General Alexander Godley, to oversee our growing army. Then forty-three years old, an ambitious and impoverished Anglo-Irishman, Godley had led a column of mounted infantry in the Boer War, and managed to distance himself from the disasters of that campaign. Otherwise he had spent much of his martial career cultivating connections to serve social and financial advancement. He was in no position to refuse the £2000 a year offered by New Zealand. For Godley the connection was make or break. Always a chilly enigma to those who served under him, energetic and ambitious, he now had the chance to use New Zealanders to make a name for himself — or otherwise disappear forever in the far antipodes. Though New Zealanders were never comfortable with Godley, nor he with them, he was soon training thousands of the country's young for the battlefield.

By 1914 Godley had some 26,000 New Zealanders ready for war. He had, he announced, laid the foundation of an expeditionary force which the country would 'clamour to send' in the event of European conflict. Godley's territorial army was inspected by General Sir Ian Hamilton, soon to become a significant name to New Zealanders, in his capacity as Inspector General of British Overseas Forces. Hamilton pronounced our human material as 'second to none', though he complained that our troops lacked 'an ingrained habit of discipline'. In public he pronounced that New Zealand and the British Empire must stand or fall together. He hinted strongly that New Zealand might one day need the Empire to withstand menace from Asia, a recurrent theme in our island story. But Hamilton had no need to dangle that carrot. As never before, as never since, New Zealand was a nation in arms, awaiting a call. What we didn't have was a war to go to. It might be seen as humorous if it hadn't had so hideous a sequel.

In 1914, as if to oblige us, distant guns were primed as one European crisis followed another. Politicians puffed, diplomats dithered, and quite suddenly in August 1914 — without anyone knowing quite how or why — vast military machines were clanking toward war. On one side stood imperial Britain, France and Russia. On the other was powerful Germany and the ailing Austro-Hungarian Empire. Within a month or two Turkey, fiercely guarding the last fragments of its once great Ottoman Empire, joined with Germany and Austria.

The war was never New Zealand's. Our territory was not at risk: we could not have been further from it all. Even the causes of the conflict were not clear to us. But Britain declared war on our behalf. We not only had no say in the matter: we didn't want one. Ebullient crowds in tens of thousands took to the streets, with Union Jacks waving. Such street demonstrations, in latter decades of the century, have been against war. But in 1914 we couldn't get into it quickly enough. New Zealanders would never embrace war so extravagantly again. From frosty South Island sheep stations, from dank North Island bush country, from goldfield and gumfield, coal mine and timber mill, office and factory, young men rode or ran to recruiting offices and sometimes fought for places in the queue. Their greatest fear was that the war might be over before they got there.

The first 1400 volunteers, drawn from Auckland and

Wellington, were dispatched within two weeks to take over the German territory of Samoa. It was a quick and bloodless affair, with the largest New Zealand loss in perspiration. Suffocatingly hot in winter uniforms, New Zealand soldiers hoisted the Union Jack over the coconut trees of Upolu and deprived German warships of a Pacific base. After which there was little to do but settle for a long tropical picnic.

The bulk of the volunteers left behind had a strong rural colouring, with musterers and bushmen and small-town boys leavened a little by schoolteachers and university students; they were drilled into an expeditionary force 8500 strong. At camps throughout New Zealand they were trained for a few weeks, then gathered in Wellington to embark in a convoy of sixteen ships. No troops in the history of the world ever travelled further to fight a war. They were farewelled passionately on Wellington's wharves. Ahead was a battle undreamt of, a catastrophe without precedent in their young country's story. For the moment, however, it was all heady adventure. They were off to see the world and save the Empire. At Albany, in Western Australia, the New Zealand adventurers joined forces with 20,000 Australians to form a still mightier convoy. The joint force would soon be named the Australian and New Zealand Expeditionary Force. The English language had a new and memorable word: ANZAC.

The Anzacs expected to fight in France. As they sailed toward Europe, Turkey finally teetered into war on Germany's side, immediately imperilling Russia to the north and the Suez Canal to the south. The Anzacs, in a swift change of plan, were landed in Egypt. There New Zealanders skirmished briefly with Turks on the banks of the Suez Canal, suffered their first casualties, trained on the desert sand, and battled with heat, flies and the fleshpots of Cairo. The casualty rate from venereal disease was soon a mortifying five per cent; many were shipped home. Anzacs, meanwhile, stormed Cairo's red-light district, the Wazzir, and all but burned the neighbourhood down. Australians blamed New Zealanders for the affair, and New Zealanders the Australians. Either way, when British military police fired upon the rioting soldiery, casualties were approximately in proportion to the two countries' representation in Egypt — there were three Australians wounded and one New Zealander.

While New Zealanders suffered the slings and arrows of outrageous Egypt, the first winter of the war in Europe was ending. On the Western Front, the British, French and Germans were fighting to a murderous stalemate. Three hundred and fifty miles of boggy trenches and bloodied barbed wire stretched from the North Sea to the Swiss Alps. Casualties were moving past their first million. In a few dazing months, Europe's politicians and generals had laboured mightily to create the largest and most ferocious war mankind had ever known. To the east, Russia's shaky Tsarist regime was reeling from German offensives, and was now also menaced by belligerent Turkey.

One who thought there was a quick way to end the war was the eloquent and obsessive Winston Churchill, then forty years old and sitting in the British War Cabinet as First Lord of the Admiralty. He offered his colleagues a tempting vision of early victory by way of the Dardanelles, the slender sea lane which divides Turkey and joins the Mediterranean to the Black Sea. He argued that the impasse in Western Europe could be ended by a vigorous flanking movement to the east — one which might knock out Turkey, relieve pressure on Russia, shorten the war and save millions of lives. It is clear that the Dardanelles were already an obsession of Churchill's. In 1898 he had written a novel called *Savrola*, which climaxed with a fleet of powerful warships forcing a path through 'a sort of Dardanelles' to win a fictional victory. Within two weeks of the outbreak of World War I — and before Turkey was even *in* the war — he was urging such a reckless venture on the British Cabinet because two German warships were sheltering off Constantinople (now Istanbul). That proposition had been rejected as too bellicose. The second time round, in 1915, his colleagues listened more carefully. Churchill was proposing the tried and true British form of gunboat diplomacy: sending in warships to fire off some salvoes and silence the rebellious natives. It had worked before. It might work again, on a mightier scale.

On 19 March 1915, eighteen British and French warships, guns thundering, pushed up that part of the Dardanelles called the

Narrows — only 1600 metres wide in places and everywhere guarded by artillery and durable Turkish forts. Beyond the Narrows lay Constantinople and perhaps the end of the war. But the Turks refused to succumb on schedule. Their mines and guns sank four Allied battleships. Turk positions were barely grazed. It was all disaster. The great ships of the British Empire, their myth of invincibility gone, withdrew speedily. Constantinople was as far away as ever. If the Turks had been taught a lesson, it was of the wrong kind. They had seen the British turn tail. Success made them a confident and forewarned foe.

Undiminished, Churchill now proposed a military assault on the Gallipoli peninsula to smash Turk guns and let the navy through to Constantinople. Others viewed the plan with scepticism. 'Damn the Dardanelles!' cried Britain's most senior admiral prophetically. 'They will be our grave.' Even then it was clear to some that it was a visionary enterprise, the brainchild of a martial romantic impatient with fine detail. Nevertheless Churchill's proposal was embraced.

In charge of Churchill's adventure was General Sir Ian Hamilton, elegant, sensitive, something of a poet, a friend of Churchill and another martial romantic. He had fought in the Empire's battles in Afghanistan, Burma, the Sudan, and South Africa. To grab the Gallipoli peninsula he gathered up 75,000 men from around the Mediterranean. Most were from Britain, France and diverse parts of the Empire, and nearly half of them the unknown, untested Anzacs. To imperial commanders they were ill-disciplined soldiers, far too casual about saluting officers, and perhaps best given garrison duty, leaving British regulars to get on with the war. Beggars couldn't be choosers; Hamilton had to use them.

With this motley army Hamilton had just three weeks to plan an amphibious assault with no precedent in warfare. The only operation one can compare with it was thirty years in the future — the D-day landing in Normandy in World War II — and there generals had two years to plan it. Hamilton would have been justified in demanding more time, more supplies, accurate maps, and reliable intelligence of Turk defences. Instead, he was impatient with junior officers who warned of likely difficulties,

103

and possible disasters. His wishful thinking began to fog the entire enterprise. He persuaded himself that the operation was just another colonial campaign. He believed the Turks might delight in British rule; he insisted that they didn't know what they were fighting for. He was soon to learn.

Since the British high command made no secret of their intention to invade, the Turks dug in deeper on the Gallipoli peninsula, pushed in 40,000 troops stiffened with German officers, and waited for someone to cross their killing ground.

Those chosen to face Turkey's guns included 4500 men of the New Zealand Infantry Brigade. The 4000 men of the New Zealand Mounted Rifles were left behind to garrison Egypt and defend the Suez Canal. Already resident in a land of fantasy, Hamilton told the troops about to make the landing: 'Before us lies an adventure unprecedented in modern war. Together we are about to force a landing which has been vaunted by our enemies as impregnable. The positions will be stormed and the war brought one step nearer a glorious close. The landing will be made good, by the help of God and the navy.'

God's role was to remain obscure. And the navy's soon proved questionable. The major thrust was supposedly to be made by British regulars at the Helles end of the peninsula. In theory they would fight up the peninsula keeping pace with naval attack. The French would make a diversionary assault on the Asian side of the Dardanelles, near the site of ancient Troy, and then withdraw to bolster the British thrust. The Anzacs were to land on a gentle beach called Gaba Tepe, about halfway up the peninsula. They were then to strike across relatively level ground toward the Narrows while picking up useful heights in the Sari Bair range along the way. It was a subsidiary role. Their job was just to stop Turkish reinforcements hitting the British at Helles.

On the evening of 24 April, a month after the British navy had been humiliated in the Dardanelles, an armada of 100 ships filled with high-spirited men sailed from the Greek island of Lemnos on the last leg of sixty miles to Gallipoli. As his fleet moved across the moonlit Aegean, Hamilton confided in his journal: 'God has started a celestial spring cleaning and our star is to be scrubbed bright with the blood of our bravest and our best.'

A nation in arms, awaiting a call. The Infantry Battalion in training, May 1914. (Jones Collection, Alexander Turnbull Library)

Their greatest fear was that the war might be over before they got there. On the way to Gallipoli, 1914. (NZ Herald)

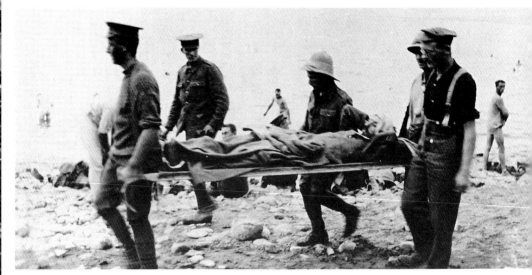

Casualties mounted toward fifty per cent of those landed.

Evacuation was cruelly mismanaged; many died unattended.
Casualties being barged out of Anzac. (NZ Herald)

That is one way of accounting for the carnage to come — the half million casualties, the 140,000 dead this confused campaign would claim. Both Churchill and Hamilton lacked interest in the details which determine success or failure. These visionaries had their minds more on winning a war than a mere campaign. It seldom seems to have occurred to them that they were thus putting tens of thousands of young lives in peril. Their neglect of detail — and of commonsense — bordered on the criminal. It would soon be seen as altogether lunatic.

First ashore on the peninsula, before dawn, at 4.30 am on 25 April, were the Australians. A naval blunder set them down not on the level coast at Gaba Tepe, as planned, but on rugged coast two kilometres north. It was the first mistake of many. It was terrifying terrain on which to land. The precipitous, often moonlike landscape is the most inhospitable on the Gallipoli peninsula, avoided even by the poorest Turk peasants. From a nameless strip of sand, a few hundred metres long, the baffled Australians hurled themselves up tall hill faces as Turkish fire began crackling around. Clutching at rock and root, shedding their packs, they clawed their way higher in the dark, losing touch with their platoons, companies and battalions. Sunrise disclosed the extent of the disaster. Though some Australians had fought their way more than a kilometre inland, struggling on into a melancholy maze of scrub and gully, many were pinned down by Turkish fire: many were in shock on the shore. In reserve, still out at sea, men of the New Zealand Infantry Brigade could only watch, wait for the first acid taste of Turkey, and wonder what was happening elsewhere.

At Helles little was going to Hamilton's plan either. Hundreds of men were being pushed fatally ashore in bright daylight. Up against Turk machine-guns — and few were needed — their blood reddened the sea. Where landings were unopposed, commanders were dithering, drinking tea, and congratulating themselves while the Turks mustered men for ferocious counter-attacks.

At the Anzac landing place, impatient New Zealanders began to go ashore at 9.30 am, five hours after the first Australians had begun to fall to Turkish guns. First to land were four companies of the Auckland Infantry Battalion, followed by men of Canterbury, Otago and Wellington. The New Zealanders battled up gullies, bashed through spiky scrub and crawled up cliff and ridge to find the fighting. Here and there, in the eroded terrain, they found thinning parties of Australians. The next bush, the next gully, might suddenly flame with Turkish guns. Yet the war was as much with the eerie, wind-whittled landscape as with the Turk. 'Hell heaped up,' one Anzac called it.

A Turk patriot named Mustafa Kemal was determined to make hell hotter. As much anti-German as anti-British, he wasn't going to give outsiders anything of Turkey. In repelling the Anzacs he would fashion the reputation which would make him — as Kemal Ataturk — the founder of the modern Turkish state. On 25 April he looked down at the Anzac landing, from the heights of the Sari Bair range, and saw a major threat. 'I don't order you to attack,' he told his men. 'I order you to die.' Die they would. Die the Anzacs did too. Turk and Anzac tussled for height after height above the beach where the latter had landed. For a time advantage teetered this way and that. By dark it was distinctly Turkey's. Turk counter-attacks beat the Anzacs back into a tight and precarious 400 acres. One despairing Anzac wrote in his diary: 'How we longed for this ghastly day to end.' For many it had ended before nightfall. At least 700 New Zealanders were dead or wounded, and more than 2000 Australians.

Out at sea, his campaign already crumbling, General Hamilton confided to his journal before retiring to bed: 'Where so much is dark, where so many are discouraged, I feel both light and joy.' There was little light and less joy in the imperilled Anzac position. Commanders composed a letter proposing immediate evacuation: 'Men,' they said, 'are thoroughly demoralised by shrapnel fire. Even the New Zealand brigade which has only recently been landed has lost heavily. If men are subject to shell-fire again tomorrow there is likely to be a fiasco.' General Hamilton was roused from slumber and told that continuing to defend the Anzac sector might mean appalling losses. He begged to differ before retiring again. 'There is nothing for it,' he ordered, 'but to dig right in and stick it out. Dig, dig, dig until you are safe.'

That was one order the Anzacs didn't need. Above the beach, on every scrap of terrain not blasted by Turkish guns, Australians and New Zealanders were digging dourly for their lives, literally for their lives, with bayonets, entrenching tools and bare hands. By morning Anzac Cove — as the scrap of Turkish coast was soon christened — looked like an overnight gold-rush town. But no one was going to strike it rich on this claim. Instead of pushing swiftly across to the Narrows, and then marching in triumph to Constantinople, the Anzacs were in an ugly and suffocating prison. Some 20,000 survivors had burrowed into an area about the size of one large dairy farm, with Turk shells exploding overhead and machine-guns felling those who risked standing upright. More, an avalanche of Turk infantry semmed likely at any moment.

As the days passed the Anzac prison promised to become a tomb. No one was safe above ground. Casualties mounted toward fifty per cent of those landed. Evacuation of the wounded was cruelly mismanaged: many died unattended. New Zealanders grew used to the sudden and violent loss of old friends and workmates.

The first Anzac attempt to leap the walls of their prison came on 2 May, one week after the landing. There were no fresh troops to put into the attack. There was no rear ground to rest and refresh men before pushing them uphill at the Turks again. All had been under fire night and day; most had had next to no sleep since the landing, some none at all. Men were dropping from exhaustion as much as from Turk bullets. Ordered to attack by General Godley — who was never to be forgiven for it — was the Otago Infantry Battalion. The battalion's objective was Baby 700, a hill so named on maps for its height above sea level. The Turks had swept the Anzacs off it on the day of the landing. From Baby 700 Turk machine-guns, mortars and snipers maintained devastating pressure on the Anzacs. To silence that fire the Otagos were ordered to scale a steep cliff face by rope at night. But the Otagos were all but asleep on their feet. After a frustrating four-hour shuffle to the site of the attack, stopping, starting, bumping into each other, many lacked the strength to haul themselves up the cliff. Those who did — those who then lived long enough to take one step toward the Turks — were mostly men doomed. There was no surprise. The Turks lay in wait with incinerating firepower; men literally burst into flame. By morning the Otago

Battalion numbered only half the men landed on Gallipoli. The 200-strong Southland Company was virtually shot out of existence. Survivors were demoralised, disillusioned, in shock — and murderously bitter. General Godley rather astonishingly reported no disaster. He insisted that the action — which gained not an inch of Turkey — revealed his New Zealanders in 'fine offensive spirit'. It was the first of many futile attacks for which New Zealanders would blame him. The Anzac dungeon didn't grow. But rough and ready graveyards did. Even then there was no rest for the dead. Exploding shells blew corpses from their graves.

Looking out on the bodies beginning to rot between Anzac and Turk trenches, one New Zealand soldier recorded: 'If their mothers could see them now, this war would end today.' But New Zealand mothers not only couldn't see them, for the most part they didn't even know their sons were dead. The long casualty lists were slow getting through to New Zealand. Anxious parents besieged politicians, demanding news, and often it was months before deaths could be confirmed. Meanwhile New Zealand newspapers were telling a golden tale. Headline-writers and cartoonists suggested that we had all but taken the pants off the Turks. There was seldom a news item to suggest that our soldiers were lethally trapped, that they were fighting to survive on an absurdly microscopic patch of Turkey. The official version of Anzac was born, one so misleading that to this day many New Zealanders imagine that New Zealand partook of a triumph in Turkey. Bitter soldiers, when the maimed of Gallipoli began to return home, had a different version, but not one that the New Zealand public, and never the newspapers, seemed anxious to hear.

The fact was that the Allied landings, promising on paper, had produced no more than a slimy abattoir; and nowhere more so than at the Helles end of the peninsula. The deeply entrenched Turks had locked and bolted the door against the British and French. The gentle, pastoral terrain of Helles had been turned into a miniature version of the Western Front, exactly the kind of stalemated battleground the Dardanelles campaign was designed to avoid. The Royal Navy was still smarting from its loss when it tried to push through to Constantinople alone. Now it enigmatically stood off from the campaign, and left the infantry to push and perish.

General Hamilton and his commanders had become hypnotised by a rather unimportant Turk-held hill called Achi Baba, which they were convinced must command the Dardanelles. Actually Achi Baba commanded nothing much, aside from some once pleasant countryside; it did not even overlook the Dardanelles. Nevertheless, in the effort to win this obscure and useless hill, thousands of men had been fed to Turk machine-gunners in abortive daylight assaults. As casualties grew calamitously, the attacks were not called off. On 5 May the New Zealand Infantry Brigade was called down from Anzac Cove to share in the slaughter. Because of stubborn British insistence on moving men forward in daylight, many New Zealanders were cut down even before they sighted the front line. There survivors were ordered to cross an exposed strip of ground, frosted with spring daisies, before Achi Baba — a place long to be cursed as 'The Daisy Patch'. It was everywhere commanded by Turk machine-guns in strongly fortified positions. The daisies were soon less conspicuous than the blackening blood of dead and dying New Zealanders as more and more were urged across the open ground. Not one of them ever saw a Turk close. Official mythology, of course, would never have it that way. Rather marvellously, and as recently as the early 1970s, a New Zealand academic with some inexplicable reputation as a military historian called the massacre on the Daisy Patch 'a thrilling charge'.

After the Daisy Patch, demoralisation and anger was as rampant among New Zealand officers as among men. Colonel Moore, of the Otago Battalion, was said to be 'all to pieces' with the shock. No one was more lucid about the experience than Colonel Malone of the Wellington Battalion, who was fast shaping as the maverick among New Zealand officers. Fifty-six years old, a Catholic, a puritan, a musician, a stickler for martial virtue, Malone was a one-time Taranaki farmer — a man who had sweated out years breaking in bush country — who had since educated himself as a lawyer. He prided himself on being a working man, a practical man, something he was soon sure his superiors were not. He had begun refusing orders which would lead to the destruction of his battalion.

At Helles, he recorded: 'My battalion up to yesterday has lost eighty killed, forty-two missing, three hundred and six wounded. Total four hundred and twenty-eight. The missing I am afraid are nearly all killed. A great price to pay for very little. I am quite convinced that the New Zealand officer has nothing to learn from the imperial man. A blundering, plunging into action will gain nothing.' His feuds with superiors would become even more bitter in the months ahead. Another sample from his journal: 'I am not hitting it too well with my superior. He seems to resent my asking for information. [Other commanding officers] say yes to everything. I am not seeking popularity.' Not among fellow officers, perhaps. But his Wellingtons were soon devoted to him. Many, and rightly, believed they owed their lives to his refusal of idiot orders.

Having sampled death and defeat on two Gallipoli fronts, the survivors of the New Zealand Infantry Brigade were shipped back to Anzac Cove. There, in their absence, the men of the New Zealand Mounted Rifles — called up from garrison duty in Egypt — had just been installed. This unlovely crumb of Turkey was even more an antipodean colony. Every lump and bump of the landscape was now named, often after Australians and New Zealanders of the original landing: Walker's Ridge, Plugge's Plateau, Malone's Gully and Russell's Top. There were less cheering names: Shrapnel Valley, Bloody Angle, Deadman's Ridge, Hell Spit.

The mounted riflemen, having farewelled their precious horses in Egypt, were distinctly afoot here. They dug in, shaping the 400 acres of Anzac into a fortress: a fortress soon, and terrifyingly, tested by the Turks. On 19 May Turk commanders decided the time had come to heave the Anzacs into the sea. Turk infantry suddenly clouded the heights above Anzac Cove; thousands of bayonets glittered. Regiments of yelling Turks hurled themselves at the Anzac line for hour after deadly hour. They only needed to breach the Anzac fortress once. Here and there the line buckled under the Turk attack. It never broke.

By noon that day 3000 Turks lay silent, dead and slowly dying, before the Anzac trenches. If nothing else, the Turks had proved themselves quite as efficient in arranging a massacre as any British commander. But the Anzacs, holding their own against the martial might of Turkey, were at last to be taken seriously as soldiers. They might seem an ill-disciplined rabble to the British, but they hadn't just risen to the occasion; they had soared above it. Never again would the Turks attempt to push the Anzacs back into the sea. Some romantic Britons began seeing their colonial cousins as young, sunburned gods. Hamilton wrote: 'There was not one of these glorious young men I saw who might not have been Ajax or Diomed, Hector or Achilles ...'

There was less room for romance in the trenches; or for jubilation. The stench of putrefying dead, after a month of battle, made the Anzac front hideous. The weak cries of the dying in no-man's-land compounded the horror. White truce flags rose from Turk trenches; an armistice was arranged to bury the dead. Turk, New Zealander and Australian mingled and talked — swapped cigarettes and souvenirs — as they went about their disgusting task. Hostilities resumed to timetable at the day's end. But with a difference. The Turk was no longer seen as the unspeakable monster of official propaganda. He was human too, as vulnerable as any Anzac. He too bled, suffered frightfully, and died screaming; he too left grieving parents and widows.

Nowhere was tension greater, or Turk pressure more menacing, than in the isolated and precarious cliff-edge perch called Quinn's Post, high among Turkish-held hills. New Zealanders managed to hold their position here on the day of the landing. Australians took over Quinn's for a time and seemed likely to lose it. Only when New Zealanders took over again was the position made stable. If Quinn's were lost, the entire Anzac sector would be imperilled. Men from Canterbury, Otago, Auckland and Wellington all served time in this nightmare. Those who survived would never forget it. Sometimes only seven yards separated New Zealander and Turk. The racket of machine-gun and rifle seldom ceased. Real rest was rare. Two antipodean innovations — the periscope rifle and the jam tin bomb — ensured the survival of Quinn's. The jam tin bomb was exactly that, an empty tin filled with explosive and all the scrap metal New Zealanders could scrounge from the beach.

Quinn's was never less than a test of character, and especially of the character of Colonel Malone. More than any commander, he consolidated and made some sense of Quinn's. He tidied and covered the formerly exposed trenches; he built comfortable bivouacs for men in reserve; he arranged latrines. 'War,' he pronounced, 'is the cultivation of domestic virtues.' He regretted only that he could not grow a few roses. He also fought Britain's martial bureaucrats to win more safety and comfort for his men. His impatience and disgust with the campaign's managers grew. He was vehemently opposed to profitless frontal attacks which British commanders ordered. And he seems to have encouraged insubordination in others. In his journal he wrote: 'If it wasn't for my good men and officers I would try and get a job elsewhere. Brigadier Johnston [has] complained about my want of obedience to orders. I went and had it out with him. I heard that a "plunge attack" by 100 men of the Mounted Rifles had been ordered by headquarters a couple of days ago. A mad fatal thing. Colonel Meldrum of the Wellington Mounteds saw the folly of it and got it countermanded. I went up to shake his hand and did so.' The Wellingtons later believed that General Godley threatened Malone with court martial.

The gap between New Zealander and Briton widened. Many expressed delight when Winston Churchill, the visionary of the ailing and failing Gallipoli enterprise, was pushed from his seat in the British Cabinet. 'The men are horribly bitter against Churchill,' wrote one New Zealand officer. 'They say we are sent here with no guns, little ammunition, no aeroplanes, and the whole adventure is a betrayal. Their language is blasphemous but deadly earnest. The organisation of this show would disgrace a sleep-walker. I cannot fathom the contempt for colonials which so many Imperial officers show.' For New Zealanders their immediate commander, the stiff, distant and unsympathetic General Godley, represented all that was wrong with the war. Meanwhile, they swore, suffered and sickened in the summer heat. In the trenches another war was being fought — against disease, malnutrition, lice, fleas and flies, and despair. Dysentery killed more men than the Turks. Many New Zealanders no longer cared whether they

The Anzacs were in an ugly and suffocating prison. Bivouacs growing on Gallipoli's slopes.

Some 20,000 survivors of the landing had burrowed into an area about the size of one dairy farm. Densely packed men at Anzac.

*"I am not seeking popularity." Colonel William George Malone
outside a dugout.*

*This unlovely crumb of Turkey was even more an antipodean
colony. More permanent bivouacs on the rise.*

lived or died. And, one way or the other, they continued to perish. Even bathing on the beach men died as Turk artillery lobbed in shells and shrapnel.

New Zealanders, and Wellington's Colonel Malone especially, looked for a way out of the trap. There was one — to the north of the Anzac position. Canterbury men familiar with the rough terrain of the South Island high country made remarkable scouting missions into arid valleys and steep gullies below the Sari Bair range. Crawling close to Turk posts, they noted that the crests here were thinly defended. They had located perhaps the only place on the Gallipoli peninsula where high ground might be gained, and a swift strike to the Narrows made. If it were to be successful, such a strike had to be soon. But the Britain's martial mills ground slowly. The simple, daring New Zealand plan became complex and unwieldy. General Hamilton wanted reinforcements from England and it was two months, the beginning of August, before he got them. By then the chance of a successful offensive had considerably diminished.

This time, for the first time, the Anzacs were central to the British plan, and especially the New Zealanders. They would mount the thrust across the Sari Bair range to the Narrows. To the left, 20,000 fresh and fit British troops would be set ashore at Suvla Bay to back up the New Zealand move. To the right Australians would rush Turk trenches at Lone Pine and the Nek above Anzac Cove. The notion was to draw Turks down from the heights the New Zealanders had to win.

There were large flaws in the plan. Too much time had passed. Surprise had gone. Colonel Malone, whose idea this had been since May, knew it was too late. 'A month ago the door was wide open,' he wrote. 'It is now shut.' Malone also doubted whether his wasted men were up to it. When he protested so to his immediate superior, Brigadier General Johnston, he was told that he, Johnston, would take the Turkish high ground by himself. Johnston owed his position to General Godley: he was also a man most New Zealanders believed to be in the grip of drink. General Godley was also impatient with medical opinion; he dismissed the views of doctors who protested that the New Zealanders were virtually all ill.

Those New Zealanders had thought this was to be a quick war; that they would soon be marching back through the streets of Auckland and Wellington, Christchurch and Dunedin, among streamers and cheering crowds; that they would soon be showing off souvenirs and scars, telling tales of high adventure in foreign parts. But in the foul, fly-blown gullies of the Gallipoli peninsula the chance of any return home diminished daily. Fatalism flourished. 'You'll want flowers on your grave next,' was the stock response to a complaining soldier. News of the impending offensive was received with a mixture of emotions. There was some lifting of morale. Anything had to be better than dying by inches in the trenches, nostrils never free of the smell of putrefying dead. And at least they might see what lay beyond the Sari Bair range; they might even see the Narrows at last. On the other hand men who had survived battle after battle now knew the odds were working against them, that their chances of surviving another offensive were small. They were right.

Central to the New Zealand plan was the capture of the summit called Chunuk Bair. From here the Narrows could certainly be seen, and possibly the Dardanelles commanded. Then the British navy could be free to push through to Constantinople and relieve tottering Tsarist Russia. The campaign might be over in weeks, the entire war in months. At least that was the hope. Viewed from the late twentieth century, the implications of success still seem stunning. They suggest that we could have been inhabiting a vastly different planet — without a punitive Treaty of Versailles, and an Adolf Hitler; without a Bolshevik Russia, and a Joseph Stalin; without Auschwitz, the Gulag Archipelago, Hiroshima and a hundred other horrors. The taking of Chunuk Bair, it is possible to argue, might well have given the twentieth century a last chance to be otherwise. At the least it can be said New Zealand has never been nearer deciding the destiny of great nations.

The offensive began on 6 August. Above Anzac Cove the Australians began hurling themselves suicidally at Turkish trenches. Nearly 3000 were to die in the attempt to lure Turks down from the heights the New Zealanders hoped to grab. That night, to the north of Anzac, 20,000 new British troops, commanded by an aged and enfeebled English general named

Stopford, began landing at Suvla Bay. Then it was the New Zealanders' turn. Sixteen hundred men of the New Zealand Mounted Rifles Brigade, and the newly arrived Maori contingent of 500 men, had the task of clearing gullies and foothills beneath Chunuk Bair, by night and by bayonet.

That night advance was an extraordinary, rather giddying success; and the only thing that went to plan for the New Zealanders in months of misery. By morning Maoris and men of the Mounted Rifles, working their way lethally uphill in the dark, had taken over a large new tract of the Gallipoli peninsula. The way was clear for the capture of Chunuk Bair itself. At a downhill site called the Apex the New Zealand Infantry Brigade took over where the Mounteds and Maoris left off, bracing for the final assault on Chunuk Bair. They had had no sleep for forty-eight hours; they had made a long and taxing climb through bruising terrain, sometimes losing their way; they had had little food and less water. By any reasonable measure, most were desperately ill, shadows of the sturdy men who landed on the peninsula four months before. Yet here they were, the heart and soul — and hope — of the entire British offensive.

The remaining 600 yards up to the summit were swept by Turk machine-guns. To the New Zealand right, the Australians were compiling huge casualty lists, but making small impression on Turk positions; they had certainly contrived no breakout. To the New Zealand left, an Australian brigade had lost its way in jagged ravines. Further left still, the thousands of fit British troops landed at Suvla Bay remained astonishingly static. Instead of pushing on to reinforce the Anzac thrust, they were brewing tea, even sunbathing and swimming, while their elderly general planned a bombproof shelter ashore. On the slopes of Chunuk Bair there was soon something of a New Zealand standstill too. Terrain and physical exhaustion had cost New Zealand the chance of a lightning grab at the Turkish summit. After sunrise the Turks had seen the New Zealanders coming, and were now in strength on Chunuk Bair.

Differences between New Zealander and Briton boiled over again. It was clear to Wellington's Colonel Malone, and to other New Zealanders, that with no support on either flank, and Turkish fire venomous ahead, the hope of taking Chunuk Bair that morning had gone. Then there was a message from General Godley's headquarters. 'Attack at once,' Godley tersely ordered. Three companies of the Auckland Infantry Battalion were pushed toward the summit. In moments merciless Turk machine-guns reduced 600 Aucklanders to 300, with shocked and wounded survivors hugging the ground; the Auckland battalion all but ceased to exist. Nevertheless the Wellington battalion was now ordered forward. Wellington's strong-willed Colonel Malone, not for the first time, begged to differ. It appears that he refused the order to advance and was indifferent to the threat of court martial. No other battalion was sent forward. The attack was called off. The plan was now to advance on the summit before dawn the next day.

All through the long, hot day of 7 August the remnants of the New Zealand Infantry Brigade crouched below the summit of Chunuk Bair with next to no nourishment, less and less water, and little real rest. They could hear the weak cries of Auckland's wounded, slowly dying after that morning's disaster. They could see the drift of smoke and dust above the old Anzac positions as the Australians continued their futile attacks on entrenched Turks. Meanwhile the great British landing at Suvla Bay, though almost totally unopposed by the Turks, produced no action at all. Any New Zealand advance had no future unless Stopford pushed his men forward. The Turks were soon massing to hit his army hard.

So already the August offensive was foundering. The New Zealanders were left to carry it alone. In the first light of 8 August Colonel Malone rushed his Wellingtons uphill. But for a machine-gun post, quickly silenced, the summit was deserted. Suddenly and marvellously, the weary Wellingtons had sight of that which they had been fighting for, dying for, month after month — the Narrows: the aim of the entire bloody Gallipoli enterprise. New Zealanders had not only taken the first significant high ground in the campaign. The smallest country involved in the war seemed to be pushing suddenly and dramatically toward the war's end. Some of the Wellingtons dug in; others went forward to form a protective screen. For an hour or two they had the summit to themselves. Some even managed time out to play cards while waiting on the inevitable Turk counter-attack.

First they were harassed by snipers, then by fire from adjoining Turkish heights. They were soon marooned on the hilltop, battling with wave upon wave of Turkish infantry, with never a hope of outside help. Ormond Burton, New Zealand's most vivid chronicler of World War I, recorded the horror and heroism of the long, bitter day: 'Every man on that ridge knew that the thin line of New Zealand men was holding wide open the door to victory, and that it must not close — must not ... So they fought to hold it wide for the host that should come up from Suvla and as they fought they waited for the crash of firing from the left that would throw off the intolerable pressure of the Turk attack — but it did not come. Men with ghastly wounds still loaded and fired, loaded and fired, while the life ebbed out of them. And in the end rifles slipped from their nerveless fingers and brave men fell in crumpling heaps.'

It was what military historians call a soldiers' battle. Officers were soon in short supply. There has never been a more desperate and despairing engagement fought in any war. Bayonet and bomb left the earth slippery with blood and strewn with fragments of flesh. There was no help — other than a merciful bullet — for those mortally suffering. There is one documented instance of a New Zealand soldier finally and reluctantly turning his gun on a dying comrade; there were surely others. By afternoon the Wellingtons were short of everything — water, food, munitions, and finally men.

The incandescent spirit on the summit was Wellington's Colonel Malone. His British superiors had never been able to shut him up; nor could waves of bomb-throwing Turks now. Time and again he led short bayonet charges to keep the Turks and their bombs at bay. 'How men died on Chunuk Bair,' wrote Burton, 'was determined largely by how men and women had lived on the farms and in the towns of New Zealand.' It certainly seemed that farmer and lawyer Malone had lived a rugged New Zealand lifetime in rehearsal for his last hours. He and many of his men, after refusing to bend to Turkish bomb and bayonet, were finally felled by misplaced British naval fire. It was the cruellest stroke of all, a blunder not atypical in any war, and especially not on Gallipoli, which had never been more than miscalculation after miscalculation. But for New Zealanders at last to take Turkey's high ground and then to be shelled by their own side was all too symbolic. For fifty years a curious and tactful silence was preserved, with survivors of Chunuk Bair too cowed and dispirited to talk of it other than among themselves, and then furtively, at reunions.

It might have beeen supposed that Malone was a perfect candidate for a posthumous Victoria Cross — now that his dissidence was silenced. He had, after all, held the always imperilled outpost of Quinn's, and thus saved the Anzac beachhead; he had taken Chunuk Bair. But the high command remained unforgiving. More mysteriously still, Malone's name was to be ruthlessly blackened by his British superiors; he would eventually be blamed for the failure of the August offensive. General Godley, moreover, didn't believe in awards to officers who were, after all, he said, only doing their job. Presumably he had the same feeling about lower ranks who were, after all, only doing the dying. The most baffling behaviour of all during the capture of Chunuk Bair was that of General Godley himself — he abandoned his headquarters and saw out much of the action offshore, from the deck of a British battleship. It has been convincingly argued that on the day he was a greater disaster than even the geriatric General Stopford of Suvla Bay.

The one Victoria Cross awarded to a New Zealander on Gallipoli went to a divisional signaller, Corporal Cyril Bassett, who again and again scurried up and down Chunuk Bair, risking shot and showers of shrapnel, repairing telephone lines. He had twice been turned down by doctors when he tried to join the army; he had worried whether he would be equal to warfare. After Gallipoli, and to the end of his life, this shy and gentle man was reluctant to admit, even to his children, that he had won a Victoria Cross. 'All my mates ever got,' he protested, 'were wooden crosses.'

Dark did not diminish New Zealand's long agony on Chunuk Bair. The thinning Wellingtons had lost sight of the Narrows, and clung to a mere lip of the summit. After Malone's death, and the arrival of dusk, men of the Otago Infantry Battalion and the New Zealand Mounted Rifles scrambled uphill to relieve their fellow countrymen — now drenched with sweat and blood, and in exhausted stupor. Some broke down and wept when relieved. Just seventy were left of the 700 who had taken the summit that morning. Through the remainder of the night, and through 9 August too, 600 mostly fresh New Zealanders partook of Wellington's torments. Again Turkish bayonets, bombs and shells failed to dislodge them; again they survived misplaced shells from the British navy. On the night of 9 August two British battalions relieved them in turn.

Next morning the British in the front line and the New Zealanders in reserve had the sight of thousands of Turkish troops storming toward them. Young Britons panicked and scattered, many running toward the Turks with their hands high. New Zealand machine-guns were then turned upon the fleeing troops, in a vain martial attempt to persuade them to fight. A number were killed. The Turk advance would be halted, but not before Mustafa Kemal had taken possession of Chunuk Bair again. It was a sad, sickening finale. Chunuk Bair would remain safely Turkish. As the last fires of the Gallipoli campaign guttered low, General Godley's drumbeating speeches won him no friends among battle-weary New Zealanders. 'The usual rot,' noted one senior officer. 'The only result of Godley's lecture was bad language.'

But Godley and the British high command were to provide one last chance for New Zealanders to win wooden crosses. After the debacle of the August offensive, commanders began tidying house, straightening the lines, making maps look neater, and in the process became obsessed with the obscure Turkish elevation, hardly even a hill, but nevertheless known as Hill 60. By late August it was seen as an impediment to safe movement between Anzac Cove and the British positions established at Suvla Bay. But there was another motive for an assault on Hill 60. General Sir Ian Hamilton had just shocked Britain's politicians by calling for another hundred thousand men; he was in need of a success to report. By now the British high command seemed to have forgotten what the campaign was about — the seizing of the

Dardanelles, the silencing of Turkey, the relieving of pressure on Russia. All those powerful aspirations were gone. British thinking narrowed to the capture of this totally insignificant, altogether worthless pimple on the Gallipoli peninsula. So all the mistakes made on the peninsula were replayed yet again. Nothing had been learned. There was little planning and next to no reconnaissance of Turk positions. Again it was a daylight attack; again it was carnage on a scale grand even by Gallipoli measure. Men of the New Zealand Mounted Rifles, many of them sullen and ill, were selected for the assault. They were shredded by Turk machine-gunners before they had gained more than a few metres of ground. After a week of futile fighting, General Hamilton reported that the action was a 'brilliant affair'. Isolated in a world where facts never dented fantasy, Hamilton luxuriated in the illusion that a significant victory had been won. There was not even a victory, let alone one of significance. Hill 60 remained Turkish to the end. Hundreds of lives again went for nothing; many wounded men died slow deaths in burning scrub.

In September the 900 New Zealand survivors of Chunuk Bair and Hill 60 were sent off to the Greek Island of Lemnos for a brief rest. They were subdued, silent, grieving for friends gone. Alexander Aitken, later to become New Zealand's most brilliant mathematician, an international figure in his field, arrived on Lemnos, and was shocked by men 'listless, weak, emaciated, prematurely aged' and with 'not a trace of animation'. They resembled, he said, survivors of an earthquake: 'It was significant that the prime cause, Gallipoli, was under a taboo and barely mentioned...I could judge equally the after-effects, by moans heard within the marquees, muffled shouts, upstartings and alarms, nightmare hallucinations...' This human wreckage was all that remained of the nearly 10,000 New Zealanders set ashore on Gallipoli.

General Godley, however, had news for them. Tactless to the last, he promised this stricken collection of men that the war had only just begun. For weary and disillusioned Sergeant Ewen Pilling, later to die in France, the general's rhetoric was the last straw: 'General Godley,' he wrote in his diary, 'did a great skite

In the foul, fly-blown gullies of the peninsula the chance of any return home diminished daily. "You'll want flowers on your grave next" was the stock response to a complaining soldier.
(Athol Williams Collection, Alexander Turnbull Library)

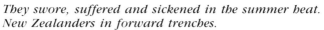

They swore, suffered and sickened in the summer heat. New Zealanders in forward trenches.

Left: *"They say the whole adventure is betrayal. Their language is blasphemous but deadly earnest."* Front-line New Zealanders.

Right: *Men who had survived battle after battle now knew the odds were working against them.*

The Anzac prison promised to become a tomb. A hastily dug grave at Anzac.

The only thing that went to plan for the New Zealanders in months of misery. The nightmare approach to Chunuk Bair.
(Alexander Turnbull Library)

Shadows of the sturdy men who landed on the peninsula four months earlier. Yet here they were, the heart and soul — and hope — of the British offensive. New Zealanders near the summit of Chunuk Bair.

"All my mates ever got were wooden crosses." Signaller and Victoria Cross winner Cyril Bassett.

The last fires of the Gallipoli campaign guttered low. Survivors, wounded and dying after the August offensive.

about the fighting done. He seems to think of us as fit as ever, pictures us in the forefront of more slaughters, and finally marches at the head of the remainder into Constantinople. I guess they are going to have to find a few more New Zealanders...When one reads of the sick and wounded anxious to be back at the front again — well, it is all piffle. I have yet to meet one. The man who says so is a skite or a fool.' Published obscurely and privately in the 1930s, Pilling's diary gives the lie to the sweet-smelling version of Gallipoli which publicly and wistfully persists to this day.

The horror of the campaign, however, had begun to seep out. Australian journalist Keith Murdoch, observing the disenchanted Anzacs, noted that 'sedition is talked around every tin of bully beef opened on the peninsula.' Murdoch travelled to London to tell Britain's politicians the worst. General Hamilton was sacked, like Winston Churchill before him. In November Lord Kitchener at last paid a courtesy call. Legend insists that when he sighted the Anzac battlefield his only comment was 'My God.' A savage winter arrived. Floods drowned men in the trenches; blizzards froze sentries at their posts. Evacuation was soon seen as the only useful strategy.

If half the ingenuity of the evacuation had gone into the campaign itself, the Anzacs might long before have been marching through Constantinople. In December men were smuggled out of Anzac nightly, brought down to the beach from distant outposts, and ferried to ships which sailed before dawn. The ever fewer men in the front line expended much ammunition to convince the Turks that ten times their number were still in residence. All the same, New Zealanders found it difficult to believe that it was over. Before leaving many found enough time to tend the graves of friends who were to remain on the peninsula, and to recall others who had no graves. On the last night the final few hundred Anzacs set mines and booby-traps to check Turks tempted to pursue them down to the sea. Ingenious self-firing rifles, triggered by a water-drip, were set working in front-line trenches. Then they crept away down silent, abandoned trench lines. Before dawn Anzac Cove was Turkey's again. Hardly a life had been lost; it was the most bloodless event in eight months of agony. A week or two later the British escaped the peninsula in similarly silent fashion.

The great Gallipoli misadventure was over. Two thousand and seven hundred New Zealanders were dead, with 5000 wounded. Many wounded eventually died too. Others would survive as physical and sometimes mental cripples. Many of those who survived intact would perish in France as World War I went on its deadly way. There would be another 16,000 dead for the nation to mourn. Per capita it would be the greatest combatant loss of any nation involved in the war. The country's loyalty to the British Empire had been established, but at dreadful cost. New Zealand would be the poorer for decades because of that awesome loss of its young.

History has little patience with losers. Gallipoli was the greatest reverse to British arms since the American revolution. It still dwarfs any other imperial disaster. It can be argued that the retreat from the spiny foothills of the Sari Bair signalled the beginning of the end of the British Empire. Britain had never been seen to back down so shamelessly before. Indian, Arab and African no longer saw the British Empire as invincible. Four decades later, after riot and revolution, they would be running their own affairs.

As for New Zealanders, the tragedy nourished a new and tender nationalism. In the 1980s that nationalism has at last become assertive, with the country reconsidering traditional connections, and defying bullying allies, but it doesn't hurt to be reminded that the rough prospectus of our nationhood was prepared in a melancholy war 16,000 kilometres and seventy-five years away. In 1915 the idea of New Zealand as a nation — distinct from Britain — was still relatively new and largely a wistful literary conception. Perhaps a catastrophe was necessary for the notion to take root. If so, Gallipoli served some purpose. The men who sailed off to Gallipoli may have gone as citizens of the Empire; those who voyaged home were unmistakably New Zealanders. For them the mystique of Empire, of Britain as motherland, had perished on Chunuk Bair.

On the peninsula today no memorial commands the mind and eye more than New Zealand's, on Chunuk Bair. On it are inscribed the names of more than 2000 New Zealanders who had no identified resting-place. New Zealanders still live uneasily with their history, still more so with their heroes. So let it merely be said that the Gallipoli campaign was not of their making; it was never their failure. No men tried harder or reached higher. In death they command the peninsula as they never did in life. Chunuk Bair may not be holy ground, but it is certainly a place of pilgrimage for New Zealanders. Listen long enough, as the Aegean wind whispers up the gullies, and sings among Turkish pines, and the dead of Gallipoli live a little again. They may well live a little forever.